ULT

Super Silly JOKE BOOK for Kids

Ultimate Super Silly Joke Book for Kids is a collection of previously published material. Portions of this book have been reproduced from *Super Silly Jokes for Kids*, published in 2020 by Happy Fox Books, *Super Funny Knock-Knock Jokes and More for Kids*, published in 2022 by Happy Fox Books, *Super Funny Fill-Ins for Kids*, published in 2022 by Happy Fox Books, and *Awesome Funny Fill-Ins for Kids*, published in 2022 by Happy Fox Books. Reproduction of its contents is strictly prohibited without written permission from the rights holder.

ISBN 978-1-64124-228-8

To learn more about the other great books from Fox Chapel Publishing, or to find a retailer near you, call toll-free
800-457-9112 or visit us at *www.FoxChapelPublishing.com*.

We are always looking for talented authors. To submit an idea, please send a brief inquiry to acquisitions@foxchapelpublishing.com.

Fox Chapel Publishing makes every effort to use environmentally friendly paper for printing.

Printed in China
First printing

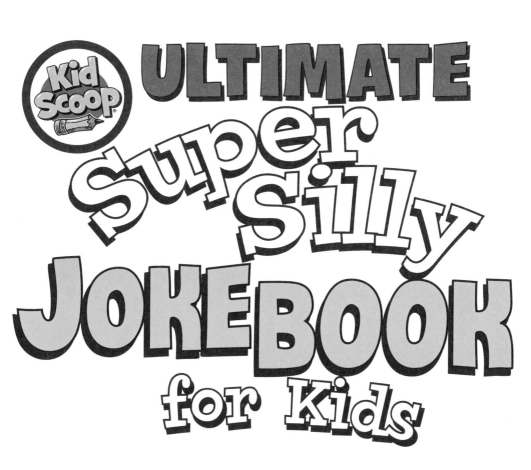

ULTIMATE Super Silly JOKE BOOK for Kids

Kid Scoop®

Vicki Whiting

Illustrated by
Jeff Schinkel

Happy Fox
BOOKS

Congratulations! You are now holding a book that will bring laughter to your world.

Q: Why did the chicken cross the road?

A: To get a copy of this joke book!

Laughter brings people together. This book is jam-packed with jokes and funny fill-in stories designed to make you and your friends and family laugh, smile, or even groan.

Try the jokes out on your friends, family, and even your teachers to bring joy to the world—they are for anyone who needs a laugh!

Enjoy!

Funny Fill-Ins

Ready for some silliness?

Complete the funny fill-in stories in this book by collecting words from your family and friends. Every time the story will be hilarious in a new way! Here's how it works:

ASK a friend or family member for each kind of word on the list. Don't let them read the story first!

FILL IN the missing words in the story using the words given to you by your friend or family member.

READ the silly story aloud. Get ready for an attack of the giggles as the crazy story is revealed to your friends!

WORDS TO KNOW:

NOUN
A person, place or thing. For example:
EGG, HAT, TREE, BANANA, COMPUTER

PROPER NOUN
Proper nouns describe a particular person, place, or thing and start with a capital letter. For example:
FRED, MRS. MULBERRY, NORTH CAROLINA, MICKEY MOUSE, STATUE OF LIBERTY

VERB
An action word. For example:
RUN, SWIM, THINK, JUMP, DANCE

ADVERB
Describes a verb. For example:
SLOWLY, CAREFULLY, LOUDLY

ADJECTIVE
A word that describes a person, place, or thing. For example:
LARGE, FUNNY, ANGRY, FUZZY, BRIGHT

INTERJECTION
A word that someone says suddenly to express a feeling or emotion. For example:
WOW! YIKES! DRAT!

Why will a shark avoid eating a clownfish?

They taste funny.

What's the favorite snack of sea monsters?

Fish and ships.

What do whales like to chew?

Blubber gum.

Why are fish such terrible basketball players?

They're afraid to go near the net.

How many tickles does it take to make an octopus laugh?

Ten-tickles.

Ask a friend or family member for each of these words. Then use their words to fill in the silly story of Reject Robot on the next page to create a Funny Fill-In to read aloud!

_____ NOUN

_____ NOUN

_____ PLURAL NOUN

_____ PLURAL NOUN

_____ PLURAL NOUN

_____ PLURAL NOUN

_____ PROPER NOUN

_____ PLURAL NOUN

_____ PLURAL NOUN

_____ ADJECTIVE

_____ ADJECTIVE

_____ ADJECTIVE

_____ ADJECTIVE

_____ INTERJECTION

_____ VERB

Reject Robot

Scientists recently developed a robot that makes breakfast

and delivers it to your _____. D.E.X.T.E.R. is
NOUN

a robot that can be programmed to _____
VERB

coffee beans, and make delicious _____, too.
PLURAL NOUN

However, initial trials had D.E.X.T.E.R. putting

_____ inside the coffee machine along with
PLURAL NOUN

_____ _____.
ADJECTIVE   PLURAL NOUN

D.E.X.T.E.R. often placed _____
ADJECTIVE

_____ into the toaster. After ruining three
PLURAL NOUN

toasters, the research team installed new _____
PLURAL NOUN

and that helped.

D.E.X.T.E.R. was programmed to say "Good Morning!"

Unfortunately, after a few days he began to shout

"_____" instead, often while throwing
INTERJECTION

_____ _____ out the window.
ADJECTIVE   PLURAL NOUN

"Well, back to the old _____
ADJECTIVE

_____," said lead researcher, Dr. Alexis
NOUN

_____.
PROPER NOUN

Knock! Knock!

Who's there?

Etch.

Etch who?

Eww! You sneezed on your door!

Knock! Knock!

Who's there?

Leaf.

Leaf who?

Leaf me alone, please!

Knock! Knock!

Who's there?

Mustache.

Mustache who?

I mustache you a question, but I'll shave it for later.

Knock! Knock!
Who's there?
Ketchup.
Ketchup who?
Ketchup with me,
I'm pretty fast!

Knock! Knock!

Who's there?

Alex.

Alex who?

Alex the questions around here!

Knock! Knock!

Who's there?

Luke.

Luke who?

Luke out the window to find out!

Ask a friend or family member for each of these words. Then use their words to fill in the silly story of Count Alucard's Castle on the next page to create a Funny Fill-In to read aloud!

_____ NOUN	_____ ADJECTIVE
_____ NOUN	_____ ADJECTIVE
_____ NOUN	_____ ADJECTIVE
_____ NOUN	_____ ADJECTIVE
_____ PLURAL NOUN	_____ ADJECTIVE
_____ PLURAL NOUN	_____ ADJECTIVE
_____ PLURAL NOUN	_____ VERB
_____ INTERJECTION	_____ PAST TENSE VERB

Count Alucard's Castle

Count Alucard's castle was a total mess. Several

_____ were floating in the courtyard fountain.
PLURAL NOUN

A/an _____ _____ was tangled in some
ADJECTIVE   NOUN

cobwebs above the parlor. The staircase was covered in

_____ _____. An expensive
ADJECTIVE   PLURAL NOUN

_____ _____ had been knocked
ADJECTIVE   NOUN

over and broken.

"_____!" cried Count Alucard. "This mess
INTERJECTION

makes my blood boil!"

"We'll help you clean up the place," said his niece

Rue, as his nephew Muerto began to _____
VERB

the entry way.

Soon, Rue had _____ through the first floor,
PAST TENSE VERB

replacing the suit of armor's _____. Muerto
NOUN

cleaned up the courtyard, planting fresh _____
PLURAL NOUN

all around the castle moat. They worked together to remove

the _____ _____ from the
ADJECTIVE   NOUN

_____ tower.
ADJECTIVE

By sunrise, the castle looked _____,
ADJECTIVE

just the way Count Alucard likes it!

What kind of fish do pirates like best of all?

Goldfish.

Why don't pirates play cards when they're at sea?

They're usually standing on the deck.

What do you call a pirate who designs buildings?

An ARRRchitect.

What lies at the bottom of the sea and trembles constantly?

A nervous wreck.

What sort of grades did the pirate earn in school?

He had a sea average.

Ask a friend or family member for each of these words. Then use their words to fill in the silly story of Spawning Season on the next page to create a Funny Fill-In to read aloud!

_____
PLURAL NOUN

_____
PLURAL NOUN

_____   _____
NOUN   PLURAL NOUN

_____   _____
NOUN   PAST TENSE VERB

_____   _____
NOUN   VERB

_____   _____
NOUN   VERB

_____   _____
NOUN   VERB

_____   _____
NOUN   VERB

_____   _____
PLURAL NOUN   VERB

_____   _____
PLURAL NOUN   ADJECTIVE

_____   _____
PLURAL NOUN   ADJECTIVE

Spawning Season

My _____ friends and I went for a long

ADJECTIVE

_____ yesterday along a _____

VERB   NOUN

that ran besides a stream. There were many _____

PLURAL NOUN

to climb and occasionally the _____narrowed,

NOUN

and we had to _____ our way across

VERB

_____.

PLURAL NOUN

We came to a place where the stream opened to a/an

_____and led to a small waterfall. It had

NOUN

_____the previous day and the water rushed over

PAST TENSE VERB

the _____, splashing as it dropped to the

PLURAL NOUN

_____below.

NOUN

We sat down and enjoyed our _____

ADJECTIVE

_____.

PLURAL NOUN

Suddenly a fish about as big as a/an _____ leaped

NOUN

into the air. And then another and another. It seemed they were

trying to _____ over the waterfall. We watched in

VERB

amazement as other _____ tried, too. When one

PLURAL NOUN

exhausted _____ finally made it over, we all

NOUN

began to _____ and cheer.

VERB

It's the spawning season, and these were salmon, trying

to_____ upstream to find their _____.

VERB   PLURAL NOUN

Knock! Knock!

Who's there?

Cannelloni.

Cannelloni who?

Cannelloni a few bucks until I get my allowance?

Knock! Knock!

Who's there?

Bacon.

Bacon who?

Bacon some cookies in there?

Knock! Knock!
Who's there?
Honeybee.
Honeybee who?
Honeybee a dear and open the door.

Knock! Knock!
Who's there?
Chickens.
Chickens who?
No, no.
Chickens cluck.
Owls whoo!

Knock! Knock!

Who's there?

Wood.

Wood who?

Wood you just open the door?

Knock! Knock!

Who's there?

Iran.

Iran who?

Iran here from far away.

Ask a friend or family member for each of these words. Then use their words to fill in the silly story of Growing Problems on the next page to create a Funny Fill-In to read aloud!

_____   _____
NOUN   PLURAL NOUN

_____   _____
NOUN   PLURAL NOUN

_____   _____
NOUN   PLURAL NOUN

_____   _____
NOUN   PLURAL NOUN

_____   _____
NOUN   PLURAL NOUN

_____   _____
NOUN   PLURAL NOUN

_____   _____
NOUN   PLURAL NOUN

_____   _____
NOUN   ADJECTIVE

_____   _____
ADJECTIVE   ADJECTIVE

_____   _____
ADJECTIVE   ADJECTIVE

_____
INTERJECTION

Growing Problems

"This can't be right," said Baxter Bunny as he looked at his garden. Instead of a row of carrots, there were

_____ _____ sprouting from
    ADJECTIVE   PLURAL NOUN

the _____. He used a/an _____
      NOUN   NOUN

to dig into the _____.
                   NOUN

Bobbi Bunny saw her brother carrying a

_____ basket of_____.
     ADJECTIVE   PLURAL NOUN

"_____!" she cried. "How will we
     INTERJECTION

make _____ stew for dinner with nothing but
       NOUN

_____ _____?"
    ADJECTIVE   PLURAL NOUN

Baxter said, "Don't worry, Sis. I have a/an

_____ idea!" He painted a sign that said:
    ADJECTIVE

"Buy one _____, get a/an _____
         NOUN   NOUN
FREE!"

_____ came from miles around as word
   PLURAL NOUN

spread. Baxter and Bobbi soon had enough money to buy

a/an _____ _____ of their
       ADJECTIVE   NOUN

favorite _____.
            PLURAL NOUN

"Who knew there was a market for _____?"
                                   PLURAL NOUN

said Bobbi as they walked to the _____.
                               NOUN

What is a vampire's favorite fruit?

Neck-tarines.

Why did the zombie stay home from school?

He felt rotten.

What does a ghost do when it gets in a car?

Fastens its sheet belt.

HARRY CLOTTER

Why did the vampire visit the library?

He wanted to sink his teeth into a good book!

How do monsters like their coffee?

With scream and sugar.

Ask a friend or family member for each of these words. Then use their words to fill in the silly story of Can Hippos Swim? on the next page to create a Funny Fill-In to read aloud!

NOUN	ADJECTIVE
NOUN	ADJECTIVE
NOUN	ADJECTIVE
NOUN	ADJECTIVE
NOUN	PLURAL NOUN
VERB	PLURAL NOUN
VERB	PLURAL NOUN
VERB	PLURAL NOUN
	PLURAL NOUN
	PLURAL NOUN

Can Hippos Swim?

Can hippos swim, I wonder? In the morning, they go down to

the _____. Sometimes all you can see are
         NOUN

their _____ sticking out of the
              NOUN

_____. Then you watch their mouth
        PLURAL NOUN

_____ and they make a great
           VERB

_____ yawn. Or maybe they just want to feel
      ADJECTIVE

the _____ on their _____.
            NOUN   PLURAL NOUN

I like to imagine that under the water, their legs can

_____ gently to keep them afloat. Except that
         VERB

they must _____ _____.
                 VERB   PLURAL NOUN
How is it that they don't sink to the bottom of the lake?

When I go into _____
                      ADJECTIVE

_____, I must wear a life vest or be inside
        NOUN

a/an _____ that keeps me afloat.
            NOUN

I imagine that even if hippos can swim, they would choose to

glide through the water on _____
                                  ADJECTIVE

_____. They might even like to try diving
      PLURAL NOUN

from _____ _____ like
          ADJECTIVE   PLURAL NOUN

graceful _____. We can only wonder.
                PLURAL NOUN

Knock! Knock!

Who's there?

Says.

Says who?

Says ME, that's who!

Knock! Knock!

Who's there?

Tank.

Tank who?

You're welcome.

Knock! Knock!

Who's there?

Purple alligator.

Purple alligator who?

Wait. Just how many purple alligators do you know?

Knock! Knock!
Who's there?
Ghosts.
Ghosts who?
Ghosts stand away from the door so I can come in!

Knock! Knock!

Who's there?

Canoe.

Canoe who?

Canoe just open the door?

Knock! Knock!

Who's there?

Adore.

Adore who?

Adore is between us. Open up!

Ask a friend or family member for each of these words. Then use their words to fill in the silly story of Haircut Hiccups on the next page to create a Funny Fill-In to read aloud!

_____ NOUN	_____ PLURAL NOUN
_____ NOUN	_____ PLURAL NOUN
_____ NOUN	_____ PLURAL NOUN
_____ NOUN	_____ PLURAL NOUN
_____ VERB	_____ PLURAL NOUN
_____ ADJECTIVE	_____ ADJECTIVE
_____ ADJECTIVE	_____ ADJECTIVE

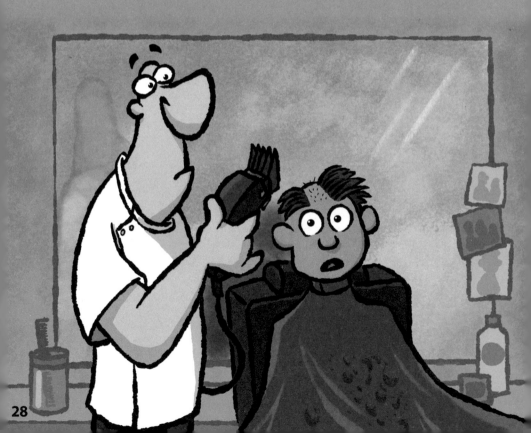

Haircut Hiccups

My friend Lawrence had the hiccups while getting a haircut.

I was joking and kidding him about it and said his haircut

made him look like a/an _____ _____.
ADJECTIVE   NOUN

It was only a joke, but it made him pretty angry. To make it

up to him, I invited him to see the _____ with
PLURAL NOUN

my family. Lawrence cheered up when he saw a/an

_____ _____ _____
ADJECTIVE   NOUN   VERB

on the _____ trapeze.
ADJECTIVE

A shiny _____ drove into the center ring and a
NOUN

dozen crazy _____ climbed out of it. My dad
PLURAL NOUN

bought us each a bag of hot _____, and a balloon
PLURAL NOUN

shaped like a/an _____.
NOUN

When we got home, I apologized again to Lawrence. "It's

okay," he said. "I can't stay mad when I think about the

_____ _____ we saw today!"
ADJECTIVE   PLURAL NOUN

And then, I suddenly hiccuped and dropped my

_____.
PLURAL NOUN

Why do nurses always have red crayons?

In case they need to draw blood.

What did the marble block say to the artist?

"Don't take me for granite."

Where do crayons like to ski each winter?

In **Colorado**.

What do painters do whenever they get cold?

They put on another coat.

What did the artist tell her boyfriend on Valentine's Day?

"I love you with all my art!"

Ask a friend or family member for each of these words. Then use their words to fill in the silly story of Path to Fitness on the next page to create a Funny Fill-In to read aloud!

_____	_____
NOUN	NOUN
_____	_____
NOUN	VERB
_____	_____
NOUN	VERB
_____	_____
NOUN	VERB
_____	_____
NOUN	PLURAL NOUN
_____	_____
NOUN	PLURAL NOUN

Path to Fitness

If you're trying to get fit, one way is to keep track of how

many steps you _____ in a day. You could
                        VERB

always get a/an _____ to help you keep
                        NOUN

count. Another way is to _____ the number
                                VERB

of _____ it takes you to walk to places you
        PLURAL NOUN

go in a day.

How many steps does it take you to get from your

_____ to your kitchen? While in your
        NOUN

kitchen, avoid opening the _____ or the
                                NOUN

refrigerator to take out a/an _____.
                                    NOUN

How many steps does it take to move from the couch to the

_____? Wait a minute! You're exercising,
        NOUN

not sitting on the _____!
                        NOUN

Do 25 jumping jacks.

How many steps does it take to get from your

_____ to the playground? Now that you're
        NOUN

there, do ten _____.
                    PLURAL NOUN

How many steps does it take to walk the bases on the

baseball field? Now that you're here, _____
                                            VERB

the bases as well.

At the end of this day, you'll be much fitter!

Knock! Knock!

Who's there?

Emma.

Emma who?

Emma bit cold out here! Let me in!

Knock! Knock!

Who's there?

Snow.

Snow who?

Snow one's at the door!

Knock! Knock!

Who's there?

Ice cream

Ice cream who?

Ice cream as loud as I can, but no one answers the door!

Knock! Knock!

Who's there?

Harry

Harry who?

Harry up and open the door! It's freezing out here!

Ask a friend or family member for each of these words. Then use their words to fill in the silly story of A Visit to the New Ice Cream Shop on the next page to create a Funny Fill-In to read aloud!

_____ NOUN	_____ NOUN
_____ NOUN	_____ NOUN
_____ PLURAL NOUN	_____ VERB
_____ PLURAL NOUN	_____ ADJECTIVE
_____ PLURAL NOUN	_____ ADJECTIVE
_____ PLURAL NOUN	_____ ADJECTIVE
_____ PLURAL NOUN	_____ ADJECTIVE
_____ PLURAL NOUN	

A Visit to the New Ice Cream Shop

A new ice cream shop opened in town last week. My family

hopped in our _____ to check it out.
NOUN

The shop had been decorated with _____
ADJECTIVE
_____ for its grand opening.
PLURAL NOUN
And they were handing out coupons for a free scoop of

_____, too.
PLURAL NOUN

We began to _____ into the shop and saw a large
VERB
assortment of _____ _____ behind
ADJECTIVE   PLURAL NOUN
the counter.

My dad ordered a sundae topped with _____ and
PLURAL NOUN
_____. Mom got a cup of _____. And
PLURAL NOUN   NOUN
I ordered a double scoop of _____ on a/an
NOUN
_____ cone.
ADJECTIVE

The shop owner gave us each a/an _____ card.
ADJECTIVE
For every 10 _____ we buy, we'll get a free
PLURAL NOUN
_____!
NOUN

What did the fog say to the valley?

"I mist you."

Why was it so windy inside the sports arena?

It was full of fans.

What's a tornado's favorite game?

Twister!

What do you get when you leave your teddy bear out in the rain?

A drizzly bear.

Match each riddle with its punch line.

What do you get when you cross a snowman with a shark?

What do you get when you cross a snowman with a ghost?

What do you call a snowman in June?

Who is a snowman's favorite relative?

What do snowmen eat for breakfast?

Ice screams!

Aunt Arctica!

Frostbite!

A puddle!

Frosted flakes!

Ask a friend or family member for each of these words. Then use their words to fill in the silly story of Homework Excuse on the next page to create a Funny Fill-In to read aloud!

_____	_____
NOUN	ADJECTIVE
_____	_____
NOUN	PLURAL NOUN
_____	_____
NOUN	PLURAL NOUN
_____	_____
NOUN	PLURAL NOUN
_____	_____
NOUN	PLURAL NOUN
_____	_____
ADJECTIVE	PLURAL NOUN
_____	_____
ADJECTIVE	PLURAL NOUN
_____	_____
ADJECTIVE	VERB
	_____
	VERB

$$123 - 19 = 104$$

$$143 - 26 = 117$$

$$199 - 99 = 100$$

$$113 - 4 = \cancel{119}\ 109$$

$$246 - 87 = 159$$

$$217 - 62 = 155$$

$$307 - 14 = 293$$

$$354 - 124 = 230$$

$$\underset{\cdot\cdot8}{} - 205 = 223$$

$$202 - 45 = 247$$

$$539 - 363 = 176$$

$$486 - 94 =$$

Homework Excuse

Dear Teacher,

My son, Eric, cannot hand in his homework today because of

something _____ that happened last night.

ADJECTIVE

In the middle of the _____ , a/an

NOUN

_____ came into our kitchen through the cat

NOUN

door. We think it was attracted by the _____

ADJECTIVE

_____ on the counter that Eric made for his

PLURAL NOUN

_____ at school.

NOUN

This morning, we found Eric's _____ in shreds

PLURAL NOUN

and the remains of his _____

ADJECTIVE

_____ all over the front lawn. We saw

PLURAL NOUN

footprints shaped like small _____ in our

PLURAL NOUN

hallway, next to our _____ .

PLURAL NOUN

We managed to _____ more

VERB

_____ but there just wasn't time to

PLURAL NOUN

_____ the homework. I'm sure he will tell you

VERB

that "a/an _____ ate my _____

NOUN   ADJECTIVE

_____ !" and he would be right.

NOUN

Sincerely,

Mrs. Klaussen

Mrs. Klaussen (Eric's mom)

Knock! Knock!

Who's there?

Ida.

Ida who?

No, not Ida-who. It's pronounced Idaho!

Knock! Knock!

Who's there?

Annie.

Annie who?

Annie thing you can do, I can do better!

Knock! Knock!

Who's there?

Taco.

Taco who?

Taco 'bout it after you open your door!

Knock! Knock!
Who's there?
Shore.
Shore who?
Shore hope you like knock-knock jokes!

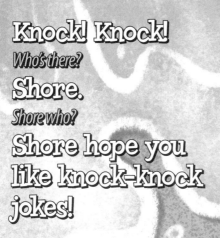

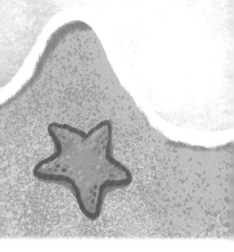

Ask a friend or family member for each of these words. Then use their words to fill in the silly story of Ice Fishing on the next page to create a Funny Fill-In to read aloud!

_____	_____
PLURAL NOUN	NOUN
_____	_____
PLURAL NOUN	NOUN
_____	_____
PLURAL NOUN	VERB
_____	_____
PLURAL NOUN	ADJECTIVE
_____	_____
PLURAL NOUN	ADJECTIVE
_____	_____
PLURAL NOUN	ADJECTIVE
_____	_____
PROPER NOUN	ADJECTIVE

_____
ADJECTIVE

Ice Fishing

Ed took his two grandchildren ice fishing on Lake

_____ last weekend. The strange thing about this
PROPER NOUN

lake is that you are more likely to catch _____
PLURAL NOUN

than fish.

It was windy as the three of them began to _____
VERB

across the _____ surface of the lake. Grandpa Ed
ADJECTIVE

had constructed a nice house of _____
ADJECTIVE

_____ and it was quite comfortable inside the
PLURAL NOUN

structure.

Using a/an _____, Ed showed Nathan and Emily
NOUN

how to cut a hole in the ice. Emily put some

_____ _____ on her line and lowered
ADJECTIVE   PLURAL NOUN

it into the _____ water. Nathan tied a small
ADJECTIVE

_____ to the end of his line.
NOUN

Grandpa Ed caught several _____,
PLURAL NOUN

Emily caught many _____ _____,
ADJECTIVE   PLURAL NOUN

and Nathan caught a lot of _____.
PLURAL NOUN

Why did the pine tree get in trouble?

For being knotty.

Did you hear the joke about the oak tree?

It's acorn-y one.

What did the pine trees wear to the lake?

Swimming trunks.

Are mountains really funny?

Yes! They're just hill areas!

46

What kind of jacket do you wear on a hike?

A trail blazer.

47

Ask a friend or family member for each of these words. Then use their words to fill in the silly story of Fashionable Spider on the next page to create a Funny Fill-In to read aloud!

_____ NOUN

_____ NOUN

_____ NOUN

_____ NOUN

_____ NOUN

_____ NOUN

_____ NOUN

_____ PLURAL NOUN

_____ PLURAL NOUN

_____ PAST TENSE VERB

_____ ADJECTIVE

_____ ADJECTIVE

_____ ADJECTIVE

_____ ADJECTIVE

_____ ADJECTIVE

_____ ADJECTIVE

_____ ADJECTIVE

_____ VERB

_____ VERB

Fashionable Spider

A beautiful spotted spider lived in a/an _____
ADJECTIVE

garden where her _____ web stretched between
ADJECTIVE

two tall _____.
PLURAL NOUN

What she wanted more than anything else in the whole wide

_____was a/an _____
NOUN   ADJECTIVE

_____to shade her in the_____ sun.
NOUN   ADJECTIVE

She _____ around the garden in her search. The
PAST TENSE VERB

flower of the snapdragon was certainly _____ but
ADJECTIVE

sadly it dropped down over her _____ and
NOUN

obscured her view.

Her friend the _____ brought her a bluebell to try,
NOUN

but that wouldn't _____ on her
VERB

_____.
NOUN

Finally, a friendly group of _____ buzzed by
PLURAL NOUN

carrying a/an _____ yellow-painted daisy. It took
ADJECTIVE

them several attempts to get it on the spider's

_____ but it perched there like a lovely
NOUN

_____ hat.
ADJECTIVE

She loved her new hat. But for the winter she decided to

_____ for a cozy, warm _____.
VERB   NOUN

Knock! Knock!

Who's there?

Goat.

Goat who?

Goat to the door and you'll find out!

Knock! Knock!

Who's there?

Wanda.

Wanda who?

Wanda stop by and visit!

Knock! Knock!

Who's there?

Amos.

Amos who?

Amos-quito just bit me!

Knock! Knock!
Who's there?
Carl.
Carl who?
Carl get you there faster than walking.

Ask a friend or family member for each of these words. Then use their words to fill in the silly story of Football Frenzy on the next page to create a Funny Fill-In to read aloud!

_____
NOUN

_____
NOUN

_____
NOUN

_____
NOUN

_____
NOUN

_____
NOUN

_____
NOUN

_____
NOUN

_____
PLURAL NOUN

_____
PLURAL NOUN

_____
ADJECTIVE

_____
ADJECTIVE

_____
ADJECTIVE

_____
ADJECTIVE

_____
ADJECTIVE

_____
VERB

_____
VERB

_____
CITY NAME

_____
CITY NAME

Football Frenzy

This season, the _____ _____ played the
                CITY NAME   PLURAL NOUN

_____ _____ in a crazy football game.
    CITY NAME   PLURAL NOUN

Instead of a football, they used a/an _____. Throw-
                                 NOUN

ing it was difficult, so they soon replaced it with a/an

_____ _____. That wasn't much better.
   ADJECTIVE   NOUN

After the kick-off, the players all began to _____ out
                              VERB

of the stadium. Fans of each team ran onto the _____
                                     NOUN

as the referees blew whistles loudly. Someone tackled a/an

_____ and another person ran with a/an
    NOUN

_____ into the end zone. The crowd cheered.
    NOUN

By the end of the day, a/an _____ _____,
                      ADJECTIVE   NOUN

a/an _____ _____, and a/an
      ADJECTIVE   NOUN

_____ _____ had been used as footballs.
  ADJECTIVE   NOUN

In the end, no one knew what the score was, but as people began

to _____ home, all agreed it was a truly
    VERB

_____ game!
   ADJECTIVE

Why did the rooster cross the road?

To show he wasn't chicken.

What do you call a chicken who tells a lot of jokes?

A comedihen.

What do you give a sick bird?

Medical tweetment.

What did the bird say when she found a sweater on sale for just one dollar?

"Cheap! Cheap!"

Why does a flamingo lift up one leg?

Because if it lifted up two legs, it would fall over!

Ask a friend or family member for each of these words. Then use their words to fill in the silly story of Charlie Loves Socks on the next page to create a Funny Fill-In to read aloud!

_____ NOUN	_____ ADJECTIVE
_____ NOUN	_____ ADJECTIVE
_____ NOUN	_____ ADJECTIVE
_____ NOUN	_____ VERB
_____ NOUN	_____ VERB
_____ NOUN	_____ PAST TENSE VERB
_____ NOUN	_____ PAST TENSE VERB
_____ NOUN	_____ PLURAL NOUN
	_____ PLURAL NOUN

Charlie Loves Socks

Charlie was a puppy and a/an _____, and he
_____
NOUN
had one unusual habit. He loved socks. In fact, if the

_____ was piled on the floor, or if one of the
NOUN

children carelessly _____ a sock on the
PAST TENSE VERB

_____, Charlie would take that sock and
NOUN

sneak away with it.

Sometimes he would _____ a hole in the
VERB

_____ and _____ it like
NOUN   VERB

other dogs would with a/an _____. Other
NOUN

times he would take it to his secret _____
ADJECTIVE

_____.
NOUN

At the end of the _____ there was an
NOUN

orchard. One of the orchard's trees had been

_____ by lightning, leaving a/an
PAST TENSE VERB

_____ at the base of the trunk. That's where
NOUN

Charlie put the _____ socks.
ADJECTIVE

With many _____ it was a warm and
PLURAL NOUN

_____ place. Over time, it would become a
ADJECTIVE

home to many other _____. But back in the
PLURAL NOUN

house, no one was able to solve the mystery of

the missing socks.

Knock! Knock!

Who's there?

Fur.

Fur who?

Furgot to tell you I was coming over!

Knock! Knock!

Who's there?

Sacha.

Sacha who?

Sacha lot of questions you ask!

Knock! Knock!

Who's there?

Sadie.

Sadie who?

Sadie magic word and I'll share my cookies.

Knock! Knock!
Who's there?

Iona.
Iona who?

Iona lot of toy animals.

Ask a friend or family member for each of these words. Then use their words to fill in the silly story of My Nutty Fort on the next page to create a Funny Fill-In to read aloud!

_____
NOUN

_____
NOUN

_____
PLURAL NOUN

_____
PLURAL NOUN

_____
PLURAL NOUN

_____
PLURAL NOUN

_____
ADJECTIVE

_____
ADJECTIVE

_____
ADJECTIVE

_____
ADJECTIVE

_____
ADJECTIVE

_____
ADJECTIVE

_____
VERB

My Nutty Fort

I had just finished building a cool fort out of

_____ and _____ in my living
PLURAL NOUN   PLURAL NOUN

room, when I heard a knock on our _____.
NOUN

"I have a/an _____ package for you," said
ADJECTIVE

the delivery guy. He handed me a large,

_____ box.
ADJECTIVE

When I opened the box, it was filled with

_____ _____. But it was the
ADJECTIVE   PLURAL NOUN

cardboard box that I really wanted. I cut some doors and

windows with a/an _____
ADJECTIVE

_____. I added the box to my fort.
NOUN

I began collecting all the _____ boxes I
ADJECTIVE

could find to add to my fort. Soon, the fort was so big I had

to _____ it to the backyard.
VERB

One evening, some squirrels moved into the fort. They

filled it with _____ _____.
ADJECTIVE   PLURAL NOUN

But they seemed so happy there, I couldn't think of making

them leave it.

Why was the jar of jelly late to work?

It got stuck in a traffic jam.

What kind of snakes are found on cars?

Windshield vipers.

Which dinosaur is the worst driver?

Tyrannosaurus Wrecks.

Who removes old road signs?

A professional de-signer.

Where do cars like to go swimming?

In the carpool lane.

Ask a friend or family member for each of these words. Then use their words to fill in the silly story of Misunderstood Monster on the next page to create a Funny Fill-In to read aloud!

_____
NOUN

_____
NOUN

_____
NOUN

_____
NOUN

_____
NOUN

_____
INTERJECTION

_____
ADJECTIVE

_____
ADJECTIVE

_____
ADJECTIVE

_____
VERB

_____
PLURAL NOUN

_____
PLURAL NOUN

Misunderstood Monster

Slugster was a monster that looked like a cross between a/an

_____ and a/an _____.
NOUN   NOUN

One day, Slugster visited the Mugtown Museum. He

wanted to check out the _____
ADJECTIVE

_____ exhibit. He had been interested in
NOUN

_____ since he was a small monster and his
PLURAL NOUN

dad had read him a/an _____ on the subject.
NOUN

On the way, when they saw Slugster, people closed their

windows to keep all of the _____ safe.
PLURAL NOUN

Inside the museum, Slugster startled the

_____ security guard. The guard began
ADJECTIVE

yelling "_____!" at the top of his lungs.
INTERJECTION

Slugster decided he had better leave.

"Wait!" said the guard. "You just startled me, that's all.

Please stay and _____ the exhibit."
VERB

After that day, everyone saw Slugster in a new way. They

would make his favorite snack at the Mugtown Diner:

_____ _____ stew.
ADJECTIVE   NOUN

Knock! Knock!

Who's there?

Ada.

Ada who?

Ada bowl of cereal this morning.

Knock! Knock!

Who's there?

Hammond.

Hammond who?

Hammond eggs!

Knock! Knock!
Who's there?
Cook.
Cook who?
You sound like a cuckoo clock!

Knock! Knock!
Who's there?
Bed.
Bed who?
Bed you'll never guess who this is!

Knock! Knock!

Who's there?

Troy.

Troy who?

Troy to answer the door faster, please!

Knock! Knock!

Who's there?

Value.

Value who?

Value ever open this door?

Ask a friend or family member for each of these words. Then use their words to fill in the silly story of April Fools' Fail on the next page to create a Funny Fill-In to read aloud!

_____
NOUN

_____
NOUN

_____
PLURAL NOUN

_____
PLURAL NOUN

_____
PLURAL NOUN

_____
PLURAL NOUN

_____
PLURAL NOUN

_____
PLURAL NOUN

_____
VERB

_____
ADJECTIVE

_____
ADJECTIVE

_____
ADJECTIVE

_____
ADJECTIVE

_____
ADJECTIVE

_____
VERB

_____
VERB

_____
PAST TENSE VERB

April Fools' Fail

Jason was always playing pranks on his friends. He would

often _____ to the park carrying
                VERB

_____ in his arms. He would carefully
      PLURAL NOUN

_____ one below every swing in the
      VERB

playground. Unsuspecting kids soon found themselves covered

in _____ _____.
        ADJECTIVE   PLURAL NOUN

On April Fool's Day, Jason finally learned his lesson.

While filling a/an _____ with
                          NOUN

_____ _____, he suddenly
      ADJECTIVE   PLURAL NOUN

sneezed, sending _____ in every direction. It
                        PLURAL NOUN

took him hours to _____ through the mess.
                          VERB

Every time he _____ one patch, he would turn
                    PAST TENSE VERB

around and find _____ _____.
                      ADJECTIVE   PLURAL NOUN

By the end of the day, Jason's _____ were very
                                      PLURAL NOUN

_____ . And even now, months later, Jason will
      ADJECTIVE

sometimes step on a/an _____ _____
                              ADJECTIVE   NOUN

and be reminded of how a prank can backfire.

Why is money called dough?

If you want to borrow money, which animal can help you?

Do skunks usually carry a lot of money?

What's the difference between fake dollar bills and an angry rabbit?

One is bad money and the other's a mad bunny.

When does it rain money?

When there's change in the weather.

71

Ask a friend or family member for each of these words. Then use their words to fill in the silly story of Playground Pollution on the next page to create a Funny Fill-In to read aloud!

NOUN	ADJECTIVE
NOUN	ADJECTIVE
NOUN	VERB
NOUN	PLURAL NOUN
NOUN	PLURAL NOUN
PLURAL NOUN	PLURAL NOUN
	PLURAL NOUN
	PLURAL NOUN

Playground Pollution

My job at the end of the day was to do a full tour of the

_____ and collect all the
NOUN

_____ that had been left behind.
PLURAL NOUN

On the slide I found a dirty _____
ADJECTIVE

_____ that had probably been left by
NOUN

someone in the kindergarten class. This one would go into the

lost and found _____.
NOUN

There were _____ and
PLURAL NOUN

_____ scattered everywhere and I was glad I
PLURAL NOUN

was wearing _____.
PLURAL NOUN

I found _____ jackets, two sweaters,
ADJECTIVE

and an odd _____.
NOUN

Someone had left their lunchbox, which had a half-eaten

sandwich. The lid was open and the _____
PLURAL NOUN

had obviously _____ the peanut butter and
VERB

jelly sandwich. One clever bird had picked up half the

_____ but then dropped it leaving a trail of
NOUN

_____ on the black top.
PLURAL NOUN

73

Knock! Knock!

Who's there?

Yeah.

Yeah who?

Take it easy! Don't get so excited!

Knock! Knock!

Who's there?

Nobel.

Nobel who?

Nobel, so I knocked instead!

Knock! Knock!
Who's there?
Heaven.
Heaven who?
Heaven seen you for such a long time!

Knock! Knock!
Who's there?
Boo.
Boo who?
Hey now, there's no need to cry about it!

Knock! Knock!

Who's there?

Roman.

Roman who?

Roman around knocking on doors.

Knock! Knock!

Who's there?

Sherwood

Sherwood who?

Sherwood be grateful if you let me in!

Ask a friend or family member for each of these words. Then use their words to fill in the silly story of Pirate Pierre on the next page to create a Funny Fill-In to read aloud!

_____	_____
PLURAL NOUN	NOUN
_____	_____
PLURAL NOUN	NOUN
_____	_____
PLURAL NOUN	ADJECTIVE
_____	_____
PLURAL NOUN	ADJECTIVE
_____	_____
PLURAL NOUN	ADJECTIVE
_____	_____
PLURAL NOUN	VERB
	_____
	VERB

Pirate Pierre

Pierre's ship sank after someone put a lot of

_____ inside one of the cannons.
     PLURAL NOUN

Pierre swam to the shore of a very strange island. It was

covered with _____ _____, so
        ADJECTIVE   PLURAL NOUN

he knew he'd have plenty to eat.

Instead of coconuts, _____ grew on the trees.
                   PLURAL NOUN

And to catch fish, he used _____
                       ADJECTIVE

_____ for bait!
    PLURAL NOUN

He built a little hut out of _____ that he found
                   PLURAL NOUN

on the _____. It protected him when rain began
       NOUN

to _____ from the sky.
      VERB

Pierre was eager to _____ home. He made a
          VERB

tall tower of _____ to catch the attention of
      PLURAL NOUN

passing ships.

It worked! The captain of a/an _____
               ADJECTIVE

_____ saw the tower and Pierre was rescued!
   NOUN

Why shouldn't you share jokes about germs?

So you don't spread them around.

When does a doctor get really upset?

When he runs out of patients!

What did the airline pilot do when she got sick?

She flu home.

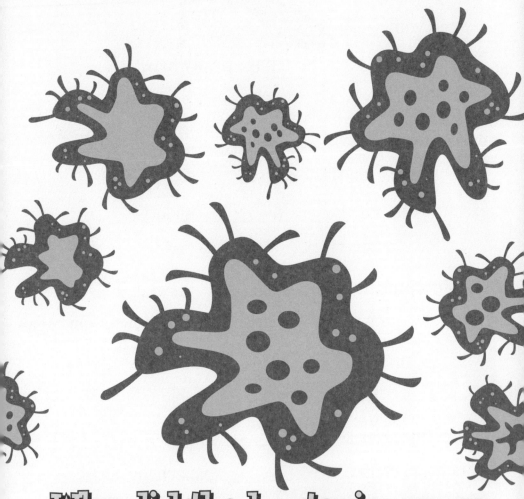

Why did the bacteria cross the microscope?

To get to the other slide.

Why did the gingerbread cookie visit the doctor?

It was feeling crumb-y.

Ask a friend or family member for each of these words. Then use their words to fill in the silly story of Lovable Ladybugs on the next page to create a Funny Fill-In to read aloud!

_____
PLURAL NOUN

_____
PLURAL NOUN

_____
PLURAL NOUN

_____
PLURAL NOUN

_____
PLURAL NOUN

_____
PLURAL NOUN

_____
PLURAL NOUN

_____
PLURAL NOUN

_____
PLURAL NOUN

_____
ADJECTIVE

_____
ADJECTIVE

_____
ADJECTIVE

_____
ADJECTIVE

_____
VERB

_____
VERB

Lovable Ladybugs

Not many people know this, but ladybugs are very

_____. They might just be the most

ADJECTIVE

_____ insects of all.

ADJECTIVE

If you _____ at them carefully, you will

VERB

often see them gather _____

ADJECTIVE

_____ and decorate their

PLURAL NOUN

_____ on major holidays. Most of us are

PLURAL NOUN

too busy with our own _____ to pay

PLURAL NOUN

attention and never notice the tiny _____.

PLURAL NOUN

Ladybugs are also excellent at making

_____ out of old _____

PLURAL NOUN   PLURAL NOUN

and _____. These are highly prized, and

PLURAL NOUN

people have been known to trade priceless

_____ just to own one of these

PLURAL NOUN

amazing ladybug works of art.

Most surprising of all is that ladybugs sometimes write

_____ things in books that aren't really

ADJECTIVE

true. Now, no one has actually *seen* them doing this, but it's

one of the reasons _____ say, "You can't

PLURAL NOUN

believe everything you _____!"

VERB

Knock! Knock!

Who's there?

Dishes.

Dishes who?

Dishes your best friend!

Knock! Knock!

Who's there?

Russian.

Russian who?

Russian to get inside! Open up!

Knock! Knock!

Who's there?

Teresa

Teresa who?

Teresa green in the summertime!

Knock! Knock!
Who's there?
Rita.
Rita who?
Rita lot of books every month.

Knock! Knock!

Who's there?

Alfie.

Alfie who?

Alfie just awful if you leave!

Knock! Knock!

Who's there?

Voodoo.

Voodoo who?

Voodoo you think it is?

Ask a friend or family member for each of these words. Then use their words to fill in the silly story of The Rough Landing on the next page to create a Funny Fill-In to read aloud!

_____ PLURAL NOUN	_____ NOUN
_____ PLURAL NOUN	_____ NOUN
_____ PLURAL NOUN	_____ VERB
_____ PLURAL NOUN	_____ VERB
_____ PLURAL NOUN	_____ ADJECTIVE
_____ PLURAL NOUN	_____ ADJECTIVE
_____ NOUN	_____ ADJECTIVE
_____ NOUN	_____ ADJECTIVE
_____ NOUN	_____ ADJECTIVE

_____
FRIEND'S NAME

The Rough Landing

The engine on my spacecraft began to _____. The
_____ VERB

warning _____ flashed "FUEL LEVEL: LOW." I
_____ NOUN

knew I would need to make a/an _____ landing on
_____ ADJECTIVE

the closest planet I could find. My co-pilot, _____,
_____ FRIEND'S NAME

located a/an _____ planet. Not ideal, but
_____ ADJECTIVE

no other choice.

The landing was tricky and would take all my

_____. I swerved to avoid some large
_____ NOUN

_____ and _____
_____ PLURAL NOUN _____ ADJECTIVE

_____. Our spacecraft slid through a deep layer of
_____ PLURAL NOUN

_____ _____ and jolted to a stop in a
_____ ADJECTIVE _____ PLURAL NOUN

cloud of _____ . We were both okay!
_____ PLURAL NOUN

We sent out a distress _____ and waited for help. I
_____ NOUN

decided to _____ outside to inspect the ship. It was
_____ VERB

dented and covered in _____, but it would fly just
_____ PLURAL NOUN

fine once we refilled the fuel tanks with _____.
_____ NOUN

Three days later, we saw the searchlights of a/an

_____ _____ in the distance. Thank
_____ ADJECTIVE _____ NOUN

goodness! After refueling, we were soon back on our way to the

Space Station for repairs and fresh _____.
_____ PLURAL NOUN

How do you watch a river on your computer?

Live stream it.

How do you know when you're getting close to a river?

You can hear it creek.

Why is it easy to work with rivers?

They just go with the flow.

What kind of rocks will you never find in the Mississippi River?

Dry ones.

What do you call all of the little rivers that feed into the Nile River?

Juve-niles.

Ask a friend or family member for each of these words. Then use their words to fill in the silly story of Classroom Visitor on the next page to create a Funny Fill-In to read aloud!

_____	_____
PLURAL NOUN	PROPER NOUN
_____	_____
PLURAL NOUN	PAST TENSE VERB
_____	_____
PLURAL NOUN	PAST TENSE VERB
_____	_____
PLURAL NOUN	ADJECTIVE
_____	_____
PLURAL NOUN	ADJECTIVE
_____	_____
PLURAL NOUN	PLURAL NOUN

Classroom Visitor

Addison entered the classroom and immediately felt there

was something _____ going on. She could
ADJECTIVE

hear the unmistakable sound of _____.
PLURAL NOUN

Under the window, the _____ had been
PLURAL NOUN

moved around. There were even signs that someone or

something had _____ in the planter boxes.
PAST TENSE VERB

Ms. Wilson's prize _____ were scattered
PLURAL NOUN

all over the floor.

Addison saw the school custodian, Mr.

_____ passing by the window. His eyes
PROPER NOUN

widened when he saw the _____
ADJECTIVE

_____ on all the desks.
PLURAL NOUN

They heard the sound of _____ rattling
PLURAL NOUN

under the sink. Carefully, Addison opened the cupboard that

held our _____ and exclaimed, "There you
PLURAL NOUN

are!" "Don't worry. It's only my friend Bandit," Addison said.

"He's been missing for a few _____."
PLURAL NOUN

Bandit seemed quite happy to have been found as they

_____ home together.
PAST TENSE VERB

Knock! Knock!

Who's there?

Lefty.

Lefty who?

Lefty key at home so I had to knock!

Knock! Knock!

Who's there?

CD.

CD. who?

CD text I sent you yesterday?

Knock! Knock!
Who's there?
West.
West who?
West awhile after soccer practice.

Knock! Knock!
Who's there?
Detail.
Detail who?
Detail of a tiger should never, ever be pulled!

Knock! Knock!

Who's there?

Halibut.

Halibut who?

Halibut we go to the movies this weekend?

Knock! Knock!

Who's there?

Wood ant.

Wood ant who?

Wood ant you like some fresh popcorn?

Ask a friend or family member for each of these words. Then use their words to fill in the silly story of Lenny Lobster's Vacation on the next page to create a Funny Fill-In to read aloud!

NOUN	ADJECTIVE
NOUN	ADJECTIVE
NOUN	ADJECTIVE
NOUN	ADJECTIVE
PLURAL NOUN	VERB
PLURAL NOUN	PROPER NOUN
PLURAL NOUN	PROPER NOUN
PLURAL NOUN	
PLURAL NOUN	
PROPER NOUN	

Air Newburg

Lenny Lobster's Vacation

Lenny Lobster was tired of the ocean. All he did was _____ all day. So he packed his
_____VERB_____
_____ and took a vacation in sunny
_____NOUN_____
_____.
_____PROPER NOUN_____

After a long flight, Lenny checked into his hotel room. The room had a beautiful view of the _____
_____ADJECTIVE_____
_____. Lenny smiled and decided to spend the
_____PLURAL NOUN_____
day relaxing by the _____.
_____NOUN_____

For the next few days, Lenny did it all. He visited the ancient _____. He climbed to the top of
_____PLURAL NOUN_____
famous Mount _____. He explored the
_____PROPER NOUN_____
Museum of _____ _____. And
_____ADJECTIVE_____ _____PLURAL NOUN_____
he even rode a _____ _____ for
_____ADJECTIVE_____ _____NOUN_____
the first time.

Back home in the _____, Lenny loves showing
_____NOUN_____
vacation _____ to his friends. He smiles when
_____PLURAL NOUN_____
he looks at the _____ _____ he
_____ADJECTIVE_____ _____PLURAL NOUN_____
brought home for souvenirs. And he is busy planning his

next vacation

to _____!
_____PROPER NOUN_____

How did the
lemon react
to losing the
race?

Why was the
grapefruit
unable to
finish
the race?

Why did the
lime go
to the
doctor?

Bitterly.

It ran out of juice.

It wasn't
peeling well.

Why did the orange get thrown out of the frozen juice factory?

Because it wouldn't concentrate.

What's green and smells like orange paint?

Green paint.

Ask a friend or family member for each of these words. Then use their words to fill in the silly story of Geese Rule the Fairway on the next page to create a Funny Fill-In to read aloud!

_____ NOUN	_____ ADJECTIVE
_____ NOUN	_____ ADJECTIVE
_____ NOUN	_____ ADJECTIVE
_____ NOUN	_____ PAST TENSE VERB
_____ NOUN	_____ PAST TENSE VERB
_____ NOUN	_____ VERB
_____ NOUN	_____ VERB
	_____ VERB
	_____ VERB
	_____ VERB
	_____ ADVERB
	_____ PLURAL NOUN
	_____ PLURAL NOUN
	_____ PLURAL NOUN
	_____ PROPER NOUN

Geese Rule the Fairway

Gordon and Gracie were Canada Geese. Their favorite

_____ to hang out was on the 13th fairway
NOUN

of _____ Golf Course. The grass here was
PROPER NOUN

the perfect _____ and with 86 of their
NOUN

closest _____, there was room to
PLURAL NOUN

_____ and _____.
VERB   VERB

As one of the _____
ADJECTIVE

_____ of the flock, Gordon's job was
PLURAL NOUN

lookout. As the others _____ into tasty
PAST TENSE VERB

_____ Gordon poked out his head and
PLURAL NOUN

_____ around for danger.
PAST TENSE VERB

Danger came in the shape of the groundskeeper. He would

_____ his _____
VERB   ADJECTIVE

_____ straight at the geese. It was his
NOUN

mission to _____ them from even landing
VERB

on his _____ _____.
ADJECTIVE   NOUN

Gordon always spotted the threat and with a great

_____, alerted the others to rise
NOUN

_____ into the air.
ADVERB

Having succeeded in his mission, the groundskeeper would

_____ on. Gordon would then sound the
VERB

_____ and the group would return
NOUN

to the _____.
NOUN

Knock! Knock!

Who's there?

Venice.

Venice who?

Venice dinner going to be ready?

Knock! Knock!

Who's there?

Isabel.

Isabel who?

Isabel working? I had to knock.

Knock! Knock!

Who's there?

Broken pencil.

Broken pencil who?

Nevermind. There's no point.

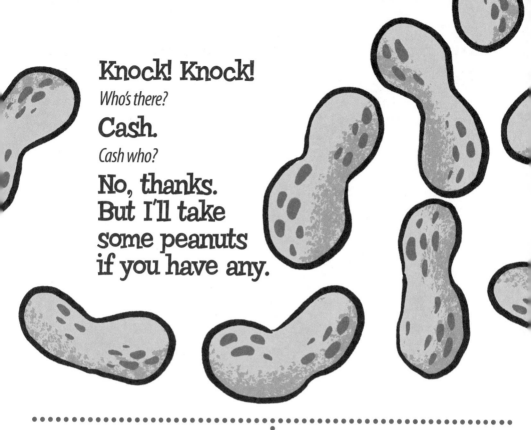

Knock! Knock!
Who's there?
Cash.
Cash who?
No, thanks. But I'll take some peanuts if you have any.

Knock! Knock!

Who's there?

Hawaii.

Hawaii who?

I'm fine. Hawaii you?

Knock! Knock!

Who's there?

Anita.

Anita who?

Anita borrow a few bucks!

Ask a friend or family member for each of these words. Then use their words to fill in the silly story of Fragrant Finish on the next page to create a Funny Fill-In to read aloud!

_____	_____
NOUN	ADJECTIVE
_____	_____
PLURAL NOUN	ADJECTIVE
_____	_____
PLURAL NOUN	ADJECTIVE
_____	_____
VERB	ADJECTIVE
_____	_____
VERB	VERB

Fragrant Finish

Last summer, our state fair held an onion eating contest. All of the contestants sat in front of a long _____
NOUN
and had a plate piled high with onions. They had 10 minutes to _____ as many onions as possible. But to
VERB
make it even more challenging, each person had to wear a hat made out of _____ _____!
ADJECTIVE   PLURAL NOUN

After the first two minutes, many of the contestants couldn't eat any more of the _____ onions. Soon only
ADJECTIVE
two _____ were left in the contest. The audi-
PLURAL NOUN
ence began to _____ loudly.
VERB

After eating five onions, Lori Fumes gave up, promising that next year she would _____ her way to the
VERB
championship.

The winner was Hal Etosis, with a total of six and a half _____ onions. He asked for some mints to
ADJECTIVE
freshen his _____ breath. When he did, the
ADJECTIVE
fresh flowers decorating the stage wilted!

How do robots eat salsa?

With microchips.

Why was the robot so tired after its commute home?

It had a hard drive.

What made the robot angry?

People kept pushing its buttons.

How do robots shave?

With a laser blade.

Why did the robot ghost haunt the graveyard?

So it couldn't rust in peace.

Ask a friend or family member for each of these words. Then use their words to fill in the silly story of School Lunch Shambles on the next page to create a Funny Fill-In to read aloud!

_____
NOUN

_____
NOUN

_____
NOUN

_____
NOUN

_____
NOUN

_____
NOUN

_____
PLURAL NOUN

_____
PLURAL NOUN

_____
ADJECTIVE

_____
ADJECTIVE

_____
ADJECTIVE

_____
VERB

_____
VERB

_____
VERB

_____
PLURAL NOUN

_____
PLURAL NOUN

School Lunch Shambles

Last Friday, something strange happened in the school cafeteria. Instead of the regular menu, they served lowfat milk, _____, and
PLURAL NOUN

_____.
PLURAL NOUN

Students had to _____ in a very long line
VERB
to get their _____ lunch. This caused a
ADJECTIVE
lot of confusion, so they were instructed to

_____ instead.
VERB

Later, Daisy Blake slipped on some spilled

_____ and her tray went flying through
PLURAL NOUN
the _____. Some of the students were
NOUN
completely covered in _____
ADJECTIVE

_____.
PLURAL NOUN

Dylan Parker dropped his _____ which
NOUN
skidded across the _____ and landed in
NOUN
the _____.
NOUN

The principal tried to calm everyone down. He spoke into the _____, but everyone was too busy
NOUN
trying to _____ through the mess.
VERB

That will probably be the last time they will allow

_____ _____ to be
ADJECTIVE   NOUN
served for school lunch.

Knock! Knock!

Who's there?

Justin.

Justin who?

Justin time! I was about to leave!

Knock! Knock!

Who's there?

Alaska.

Alaska who?

Alaska gain. Can you open up?

Knock! Knock!
Who's there?
Alpaca.
Alpaca who?
Alpaca suitcase, you fill up the car.

Knock! Knock!
Who's there?
A herd.
A herd who?
A herd you were back in town and I wanted to pay a visit.

Knock! Knock!

Who's there?

Comb.

Comb who?

Comb open the door, you'll see.

Knock! Knock!

Who's there?

Spell.

Spell who?

W-H-O. Now can I come in?

Ask a friend or family member for each of these words. Then use their words to fill in the silly story of My Cat Misty on the next page to create a Funny Fill-In to read aloud!

_____ NOUN	_____ ADJECTIVE
_____ NOUN	_____ ADJECTIVE
_____ NOUN	_____ ADJECTIVE
_____ NOUN	_____ ADJECTIVE
_____ NOUN	_____ ADJECTIVE
_____ NOUN	_____ VERB
_____ NOUN	_____ PLURAL NOUN
_____ NOUN	
_____ PLURAL NOUN	

My Cat Misty

The clock chimes twelve times as my cat walks softly up the

_____. Late at night, Misty loves to
PLURAL NOUN

_____ around the _____. It is
VERB   NOUN

Halloween night, and she's still excited from all the

_____ trick-or-treaters she saw.
ADJECTIVE

Misty loves Halloween. From her perch in the front

_____, she will watch all the
NOUN

_____ _____ as they come to our
ADJECTIVE   PLURAL NOUN

door. She is not afraid of these _____ visitors.
ADJECTIVE

Tonight, Misty is wide awake, listening to the

_____ in the trees. The _____ is
NOUN   NOUN

bright, casting Misty's shadow on the _____ of
NOUN

my bedroom. Once she has finished looking around the

_____, she will curl up on my
NOUN

_____ by my feet, purring happily.
NOUN

I know that some people think _____ cats are
ADJECTIVE

unlucky, but not me. Misty is an important member of our

_____! Having a pet like Misty is a/an
NOUN

_____ treat.
ADJECTIVE

How do farmers count their cattle?

What did the coach say to the herd of dairy cows?

How do cows keep up with current events?

With a cowculator.

"Get on the field and give me 2%!"

With the moospaper.

Where do cows go for lunch?

The calfeteria.

110

What did the farmer tell the cows when he caught them grazing in the middle of the night?

"It's pasture bedtime!"

Ask a friend or family member for each of these words. Then use their words to fill in the silly story of Tide Pooling on the next page to create a Funny Fill-In to read aloud!

NOUN

NOUN

NOUN

NOUN

PLURAL NOUN

PLURAL NOUN

ADJECTIVE

ADJECTIVE

ADJECTIVE

VERB

PAST TENSE VERB

PAST TENSE VERB

PLURAL NOUN

PLURAL NOUN

PLURAL NOUN

PROPER NOUN

Tide Pooling

Patrick and Lily loved exploring tide pools.

Patrick liked to collect _____
                                    ADJECTIVE
_____ in his _____.
         PLURAL NOUN   NOUN

Lily liked the sea urchins although she was

_____ to _____ them.
         ADJECTIVE   VERB
She also hoped to find a star fish.

They were both absorbed in watching the tide pools when a

huge _____ washed in and over the
                 NOUN
_____. It knocked them off their
         PLURAL NOUN

_____ and their _____
         PLURAL NOUN   PLURAL NOUN
flew through the air.

Patrick discovered that a real crab was

_____ on his _____. He
     PAST TENSE VERB   NOUN
got up very slowly so he wouldn't be _____
                                          PAST TENSE VERB
by those tiny _____.
                    PLURAL NOUN

Lily was _____ because a real sea
                 ADJECTIVE
_____ had landed just in front of her. She
         NOUN
carefully picked it up and stroked its back. She called it

_____ and carefully placed in back in the
     PROPER NOUN
tide pool in front of her.

115

Ask a friend or family member for each of these words. Then use their words to fill in the silly story of Dee Dee on a Roll on the next page to create a Funny Fill-In to read aloud!

_____ NOUN	_____ ADJECTIVE
_____ NOUN	_____ ADJECTIVE
_____ NOUN	_____ ADJECTIVE
_____ PLURAL NOUN	_____ ADJECTIVE
_____ PLURAL NOUN	_____ ADJECTIVE
_____ PLURAL NOUN	_____ VERB
_____ INTERJECTION	_____ VERB

Dee Dee on a Roll

Dee Dee was a dung beetle who dreamed of bigger and better things. She wanted to _____ with
_____ VERB
PLURAL NOUN
and _____ amongst the
VERB
_____.
PLURAL NOUN

But those were pretty big dreams for a little dung beetle. Poor Dee Dee thought she might never get her chance to become a/an _____ _____.
ADJECTIVE   NOUN

"You have _____ of elephant dung as far as
PLURAL NOUN
the _____ can see!" said Dee Dee's father.
NOUN
"Stop wasting *time* and start minding *waste!*"

One afternoon, Dee Dee saw a bright, _____
ADJECTIVE
object in the _____. It was a marble!
NOUN

Dee Dee became quite skilled and eventually entered a marble competition. She performed _____
ADJECTIVE
tricks and scored the highest of all.

"_____!" she shouted during her victory
INTERJECTION
speech. "I've gone from the _____ bottom to
ADJECTIVE
the _____ top!"
ADJECTIVE

How can you tell when your clock is hungry?

It'll go back four seconds.

What do you get when you mix a chicken and a clock?

A cluck.

What do you call a belt made of clocks?

A waist of time.

Why was the clock sad when the family left the house each day?

It had no one to tock to.

118

What did the second hand on the clock say to the hour hand?

"I'll be back in a minute!"

Ask a friend or family member for each of these words. Then use their words to fill in the silly story of Pinky the Pig on the next page to create a Funny Fill-In to read aloud!

_____   _____
NOUN   NOUN

_____   _____
NOUN   VERB

_____   _____
NOUN   VERB

_____   _____
NOUN   VERB

_____   _____
NOUN   VERB

_____
ADJECTIVE

120

Pinky the Pig

Pinky the pig had a problem. He just couldn't stop sneezing.

He sneezed in his _____. He sneezed in
NOUN

his _____. He even sneezed in his
NOUN

_____.
NOUN

Finally, Farmer Foxtail decided he had to do something

about this. Pinky was getting skinny, and the other pigs

would not _____ near him.
VERB

It took a while for the vet, Dr. Dawson, to even get close to

Pinky. Every time he tried to _____ him,
VERB

Pinky sneezed and ran off snorting.

The only solution was to make Pinky

_____. So, Dr. Dawson very quietly
VERB

snuck up behind Pinky and jabbed him in the

_____ _____. Pinky
ADJECTIVE   NOUN

started to _____ and then crashed to the
VERB

_____.
NOUN

Carefully the vet approached and started to examine Pinky.

"I found it!" he yelled as he pulled a large

_____ out of Pinky's
NOUN

_____. Pinky slept for the next four
NOUN

hours and awoke happy and without sneezing.

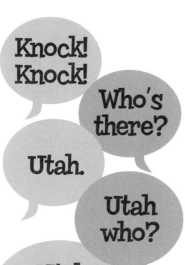

Knock! Knock!

Who's there?

Utah.

Utah who?

Utah king to me?

Knock! Knock!

Who's there?

Jess.

Jess who?

Jess me and a few of my friends!

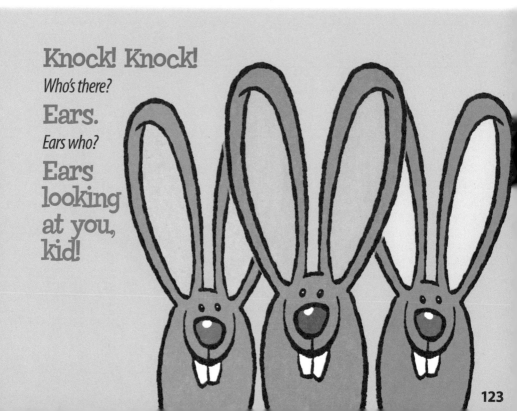

Knock! Knock!
Who's there?
Ears.
Ears who?
Ears looking at you, kid!

Ask a friend or family member for each of these words. Then use their words to fill in the silly story of Weird Watercolors on the next page to create a Funny Fill-In to read aloud!

_____	_____
NOUN	PLURAL VOUN
_____	_____
NOUN	PLURAL VOUN
_____	_____
PROPER NOUN	VERB
_____	_____
PLURAL NOUN	ADJECTIVE
_____	_____
PLURAL NOUN	ADJECTIVE
_____	_____
PLURAL NOUN	ADJECTIVE
_____	_____
PLURAL NOUN	ADJECTIVE
_____	_____
PLURAL NOUN	ADJECTIVE
_____	_____
PLURAL NOUN	ADJECTIVE

Weird Watercolors

Our art teacher, Mr. Fresco, is very creative. And a little odd. He creates watercolor paints by mixing equal parts _____
PLURAL NOUN
and _____. And instead of watercolor paper, he
PLURAL NOUN
encourages students to paint on _____
ADJECTIVE
_____ while using a/an _____ rather
PLURAL NOUN   NOUN
than a/an _____ paint brush.
ADJECTIVE

Mr. Fresco substitutes _____ filled with
PLURAL NOUN
_____ _____ for bowls of fruit.
ADJECTIVE   PLURAL NOUN

Each spring, student watercolor paintings are displayed in the school _____. The show attracts art lovers from
NOUN
miles around to _____ to see this
VERB
_____ student artwork. Last year some of the
ADJECTIVE
paintings were featured in *Modern* _____ magazine.
PROPER NOUN

Next year, Mr. Fresco will also teach sculpture using
_____ _____ and
ADJECTIVE   PLURAL NOUN
_____ _____. And while that's
ADJECTIVE   PLURAL NOUN
sure to get messy, there's no doubt the _____
PLURAL NOUN
will be amazing!

What do you get when you mix an alien and a kangaroo?

A Mars-supial.

How do you throw a surprise party for an alien?

You have to planet.

What is a space alien's favorite snack?

Rocket chips.

What did the alien say to the garden?

"Take me to your weeder!"

What do you call a spaceship with a bacon pilot?

An Unidentified Frying Object.

Ask a friend or family member for each of these words. Then use their words to fill in the silly story of Tree House Home on the next page to create a Funny Fill-In to read aloud!

_____ NOUN	_____ ADJECTIVE
_____ NOUN	_____ ADJECTIVE
_____ NOUN	_____ ADJECTIVE
_____ NOUN	_____ ADJECTIVE
_____ NOUN	_____ PAST TENSE VERB
_____ NOUN	_____ PLURAL NOUN
_____ NOUN	_____ PLURAL NOUN
_____ PLURAL NOUN	_____ PLURAL NOUN

Tree House Home

It took _____ for my dad to build our
                    PLURAL NOUN

treehouse. We were not allowed to be near him as he was

building in case he said _____
                                    ADJECTIVE

_____.
        PLURAL NOUN

When it was _____, we were so excited. It
                    ADJECTIVE

had _____ and a roof and to get into it he
        PLURAL NOUN

used a/an _____ ladder. To make it our very
                    ADJECTIVE

own, we put in a/an _____
                              NOUN

and two _____.
                PLURAL NOUN

Later that summer, we had planned a/an

_____ outing to the zoo. We packed a/an
            NOUN

_____ and were ready to go but my brother
            NOUN

Derek was missing. We called his name, checked his

_____, and looked all around the
            NOUN

_____ but there was no sign of him.
            NOUN

Finally, I climbed the _____ and
                                    NOUN

_____ into the treehouse. There he was,
    PAST TENSE VERB

fast asleep. He had taken up his _____
                                                ADJECTIVE

_____ and had decided to make
            NOUN

it his bedroom.

Knock! Knock!

Who's there?

Luke.

Luke who?

Luke through the peephole!

Knock! Knock!

Who's there?

Beef.

Beef who?

Beef-ore I freeze, can you open up?

Knock! Knock!
Who's there?
Who Who.
Who Who who?
Santa Claus, is that you?

Ask a friend or family member for each of these words. Then use their words to fill in the silly story of Hilarious Hoops on the next page to create a Funny Fill-In to read aloud!

_____
NOUN

_____
NOUN

_____
NOUN

_____
NOUN

_____
NOUN

_____
NOUN

_____
PROPER NOUN

_____
ADJECTIVE

_____
ADJECTIVE

_____
PLURAL NOUN

_____
PLURAL NOUN

_____
PLURAL NOUN

_____
PLURAL NOUN

Hilarious Hoops

My dad is a big basketball fan. His favorite team is the

_____. They're an unusual team, to say the least.
PROPER NOUN

Their mascot is a purple _____ with a/an
NOUN

_____ on its jersey. It dribbles a/an
NOUN

_____ _____!
ADJECTIVE   NOUN

Most basketball teams don't ride in a/an _____ to
NOUN

games, but my dad's team does.

Before each game, they toss lots of _____ to their
PLURAL NOUN

fans in the arena. The referee sounds the _____
NOUN

and then the game begins. If a/an _____ lands in
NOUN

the seats, a fan gets to take it home!

Dad takes me to the games as often as he can. We usually sit in

the top row with _____ and _____
PLURAL NOUN   PLURAL NOUN

for snacks.

I don't know if they'll ever win a championship, but if there is

ever an award for the team with the most _____
ADJECTIVE

_____, no other team stands a chance!
PLURAL NOUN

What did the elephant do when she hurt her toe?

She called a tow truck.

How do you know when there's an elephant in the refrigerator?

The door won't close.

What's the difference between an elephant and an apple?

The apple is red.

Why did the elephant wear red sneakers?

So it could hide in the strawberry patch.

What do you call an elephant that won't take a bath?

Smellyphant!

Ask a friend or family member for each of these words. Then use their words to fill in the silly story of End of the Rainbow on the next page to create a Funny Fill-In to read aloud!

_____ NOUN	_____ ADJECTIVE
_____ NOUN	_____ ADJECTIVE
_____ NOUN	_____ ADJECTIVE
_____ NOUN	_____ ADJECTIVE
_____ NOUN	_____ VERB
_____ NOUN	_____ VERB
_____ PLURAL NOUN	_____ VERB
_____ ADJECTIVE	_____ VERB
_____ VERB	

End of the Rainbow

Patrick had heard in class that there was a pot of gold at the end of a rainbow. His teacher had said it, so it must be right.

The very next _____ day, a/an
                              ADJECTIVE

_____ rainbow appeared in all its lovely
        ADJECTIVE

_____. The sun continued to
           PLURAL NOUN

_____ on one side of the sky, but where the
      VERB

_____ came down, the arc showed quite clearly.
      NOUN

It was so clear that Patrick was sure he could

_____ to where it seemed to
        VERB

_____ the ground. He began to
        VERB

_____ down the street and into the park. It was
    VERB

just across the _____
                      ADJECTIVE

_____. Every time he thought he was going
      NOUN

to reach it, it seemed to _____ away from him.
                        VERB

Then, it was gone completely.

He didn't want to give up. He went to the

_____ where he thought it had touched
      NOUN

down. There, in the _____, was a green
                NOUN

_____. He picked it up and turned it over.
    NOUN

The _____ _____ was
     ADJECTIVE   NOUN

golden. Well, it wasn't exactly a pot of gold, but a treasure for a

_____ collector.
     ADJECTIVE

137

Knock! Knock!

Who's there?

Fiddle.

Fiddle who?

Fiddle make you happy, I'll let myself in!

Knock! Knock!

Who's there?

Wendy.

Wendy who?

Wendy door is open I don't need to knock.

Knock! Knock!
Who's there?
Hippo.
Hippo who?
Hippo birthday to you!

Ask a friend or family member for each of these words. Then use their words to fill in the silly story of Toy Factory Trouble on the next page to create a Funny Fill-In to read aloud!

_____
NOUN

_____
PLURAL NOUN

_____
PLURAL NOUN

_____
PLURAL NOUN

_____
PLURAL NOUN

_____
PLURAL NOUN

_____
PAST TENSE VERB

_____
ADJECTIVE

_____
ADJECTIVE

_____
ADJECTIVE

_____
ADJECTIVE

_____
ADJECTIVE

_____
VERB

_____
VERB

Toy Factory Trouble

It was a very strange day at the toy factory, which began
with a truckload of _____ being delivered to
PLURAL NOUN
the loading dock.

Later, the paint department accidentally filled their
airbrushes with _____ _____.
ADJECTIVE   PLURAL NOUN
Toy robots began to _____ off the assembly
VERB
line, while several dolls had a/an _____
ADJECTIVE
_____ where their heads should be.
NOUN

Production stopped while workers _____
PAST TENSE VERB
throughout the factory, searching for _____.
PLURAL NOUN

By the end of the day, there were dozens of
_____ _____ and shelf after
ADJECTIVE   PLURAL NOUN
shelf of _____ _____.
ADJECTIVE   PLURAL NOUN

"Well, maybe we can _____ all these
VERB
_____ toys on April Fools' Day," said the toy
ADJECTIVE
factory chief.

Why did the mermaid cross the ocean?

To get to the other tide.

Are mermaids really strong enough to carry a house?

Only if it's a lighthouse.

Why won't clams lend money to mermaids?

Because they're shellfish.

How do mermaids always know exactly how much they weigh?

They bring their scales with them everywhere.

How do mermaids communicate over long distances?

They call each other on their shellphones.

Ask a friend or family member for each of these words. Then use their words to fill in the silly story of Sugar Search on the next page to create a Funny Fill-In to read aloud!

_____
NOUN

_____
NOUN

_____
NOUN

_____
NOUN

_____
NOUN

_____
NOUN

_____
NOUN

_____
NOUN

_____
NOUN

_____
PAST TENSE VERB

_____
ADJECTIVE

_____
ADJECTIVE

_____
ADJECTIVE

_____
ADJECTIVE

_____
ADJECTIVE

_____
ADJECTIVE

_____
PAST TENSE VERB

_____
PAST TENSE VERB

_____
PAST TENSE VERB

_____
PAST TENSE VERB

Sugar Search

A family of squirrels lived inside a/an _____
ADJECTIVE
tree. They enjoyed acorns, but wanted to add a little sweetener.

Sylvester Squirrel thought he knew how. He began by scratching
the _____ of the _____
NOUN   ADJECTIVE
maple just as his _____ had told him. He
NOUN
was convinced he'd done the right thing. He grabbed a/an

_____ piece of _____
ADJECTIVE   NOUN
to use as a straw and _____ it into the hole
PAST TENSE VERB
he had made.

He waited and waited. Nothing happened. He shook the

_____ and then
NOUN

_____ it. Maybe it was a/an
PAST TENSE VERB

_____ tree. Maybe
ADJECTIVE

the_____ didn't run in the winter. He
NOUN

_____ to his home as hungry for
PAST TENSE VERB

_____ _____ as he could be.
ADJECTIVE   NOUN

The next morning, his sister Sally _____ by
PAST TENSE VERB

the tree with a/an _____
ADJECTIVE

_____ on her face. In the early morning
NOUN

_____, the water from the sap had
NOUN

evaporated and left a trail of _____ all the
NOUN

way down the bark. She _____ the sugar all
PAST TENSE VERB

morning, which by now was nearly all gone.

Knock! Knock!

Who's there?

Stew.

Stew who?

Stew late for so many questions.

Knock! Knock!

Who's there?

Todd A.

Todd A. who?

Todd A. is your lucky day!

Knock! Knock!
Who's there?
Sadie.
Sadie who?
Sadie magic word and I'll tell you!

Ask a friend or family member for each of these words. Then use their words to fill in the silly story of Rocket Scientists on the next page to create a Funny Fill-In to read aloud!

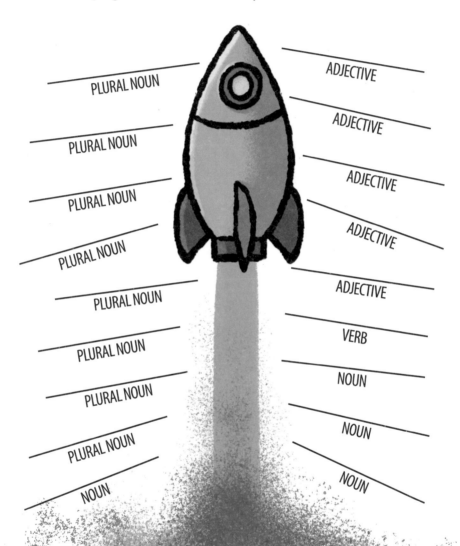

PLURAL NOUN

PLURAL NOUN

PLURAL NOUN

PLURAL NOUN

PLURAL NOUN

PLURAL NOUN

PLURAL NOUN

PLURAL NOUN

NOUN

ADJECTIVE

ADJECTIVE

ADJECTIVE

ADJECTIVE

ADJECTIVE

VERB

NOUN

NOUN

NOUN

Rocket Scientists

The scientists at Kid Scoop Laboratories performed a very unusual rocket experiment. They filled a/an

_____ _____ with a gallon of
ADJECTIVE   NOUN

_____, a cup of _____, and a small
PLURAL NOUN   PLURAL NOUN

amount of _____ to make their rocket.
                    PLURAL NOUN

As you would expect, it didn't _____ very
                                                    VERB

well at all.

They constructed a new rocket powered by

_____ and freeze-dried _____. The
PLURAL NOUN   PLURAL NOUN

rocket crashed into a crate of _____.
                                              PLURAL NOUN

Finally, using soda pop and mints, they were able to launch

a/an _____ 20 feet into the air. They added more
              NOUN

soda pop, more mints, and soon the sky was filled with flying

objects such as a/an _____ _____,
                                    ADJECTIVE   NOUN

a/an _____ _____, and dozens of
              ADJECTIVE   NOUN

_____ _____! It took several days
        ADJECTIVE   PLURAL NOUN

to clean up the lab, which was covered

in _____ _____.
          ADJECTIVE   PLURAL NOUN

Why did the scarecrow skip lunch and dinner?

He was stuffed.

Why was the scarecrow unhappy working in the cornfields?

It was for the birds.

What is a scarecrow's favorite fruit?

Strawberries.

How do you fix a hole in a scarecrow's clothes?

With a pumpkin patch.

Why didn't the kernels leave the popper?

They were cornfused.

Ask a friend or family member for each of these words. Then use their words to fill in the silly story of First Day of School on the next page to create a Funny Fill-In to read aloud!

_____
NOUN

_____
NOUN

_____
NOUN

_____
NOUN

_____
NOUN

_____
PLURAL NOUN

_____
PLURAL NOUN

_____
PLURAL NOUN

_____
PROPER NOUN

_____
PAST TENSE VERB

_____
ADJECTIVE

_____
ADJECTIVE

_____
ADJECTIVE

_____
ADJECTIVE

_____
ADJECTIVE

_____
ADJECTIVE

_____
VERB

_____
VERB

_____
VERB

First Day of School

I had a new backpack that was clean,

_____ clothes, even new
       ADJECTIVE

_____.
       PLURAL NOUN

It had been hard to _____ the night
       VERB

before as I was both _____ and
       ADJECTIVE

_____. My best friend,
       ADJECTIVE

_____, would be with me in our
       PROPER NOUN

_____ 2nd grade class and we were both
       ADJECTIVE

looking forward to meeting our _____
       ADJECTIVE

_____ Mrs. Pugh.
       NOUN

I told mom I wanted to get there early to make sure I knew

which _____ to go to and to see the new
       NOUN

playground _____ put in during the
       NOUN

school _____.
       PLURAL NOUN

When we arrived, we were FIRST to

_____ at the drop off. That was good
       VERB

because some days we could _____ 20
       VERB

minutes in line. I _____ out while Mom
       PAST TENSE VERB

went to park the _____.
       NOUN

It was strange. There was no one there. Not in the

_____ and not by the
       NOUN

_____. Mom appeared with a
       PLURAL NOUN

_____ look on her face. "School doesn't
       ADJECTIVE

start until tomorrow!" she said.

Knock! Knock!

Who's there?

Nose.

Nose who?

Nose body knows more jokes than me!

Knock! Knock!

Who's there?

Barbie.

Barbie who?

Barbie Q some burgers this weekend.

Knock! Knock!

Who's there?

Tish.

Tish who?

No, thanks. I brought a handkerchief!

Ask a friend or family member for each of these words. Then use their words to fill in the silly story of The Astounding Klumzee on the next page to create a Funny Fill-In to read aloud!

_____
NOUN

_____
NOUN

_____
NOUN

_____
NOUN

_____
PLURAL NOUN

_____
PLURAL NOUN

_____
PLURAL NOUN

_____
PLURAL NOUN

_____
PLURAL NOUN

_____
PLURAL NOUN

_____
PLURAL NOUN

_____
PLURAL NOUN

_____
VERB

_____
ADJECTIVE

_____
ADJECTIVE

_____
ADJECTIVE

_____
ADJECTIVE

The Astounding Klumzee

The Astounding Klumzee performs at kids' birthday

_____. His magic tricks are unlike any you've seen.
PLURAL NOUN

Cards and rabbits? Not Klumzee. He makes _____
PLURAL NOUN

float out of a large _____. Next, several
NOUN

_____ _____ appear, each juggling
ADJECTIVE   PLURAL NOUN

_____ _____. But that's only the
ADJECTIVE   PLURAL NOUN

beginning of The Astounding Klumzee's show!

While blindfolded and riding a miniature _____,
NOUN

Klumzee sketches portraits of well-known _____.
PLURAL NOUN

Instead of balloon animals, Klumzee makes sculptures out of

_____ _____, tape, and lots and lots
ADJECTIVE   PLURAL NOUN

of _____!
PLURAL NOUN

Klumzee's big finish is truly astounding. While a choir of trained

parrots sing "Happy Birthday," Klumzee uses a/an

_____ to neatly _____ the child's
NOUN   VERB

cake into _____ pieces. Large scoops of ice cream
ADJECTIVE

magically appear from a tiny _____ as The
NOUN

Astounding Klumzee disappears in a cloud of

_____!
PLURAL NOUN

What's as big as a cowboy but weighs nothing at all?

His shadow.

How did the cowboy get so rich?

He got a few bucks from his horse every day.

Why do cowboys ride horses?

Because they're too heavy to carry!

Where do cowboys cook their chili?

On the range.

Why did the horse always chew with its mouth open?

It had bad stable manners.

Ask a friend or family member for each of these words. Then use their words to fill in the silly story of I Miss My Snowman on the next page to create a Funny Fill-In to read aloud!

_____	_____
NOUN	INTERJECTION
_____	_____
NOUN	ADJECTIVE
_____	_____
PLURAL NOUN	ADJECTIVE
_____	_____
PLURAL NOUN	ADJECTIVE
_____	_____
PLURAL NOUN	VERB
_____	_____
PLURAL NOUN	VERB
_____	_____
PLURAL NOUN	VERB

I Miss My Snowman

Last winter, I was building a snowman out of

_____. The wind began to
_{PLURAL NOUN}

_____ and right before my eyes, the
_{VERB}

snowman began to _____!
_{VERB}

He asked me lots of questions about

_____ and _____.
_{PLURAL NOUN}   _{PLURAL NOUN}

The snowman said he was thirsty and asked for a glass of

_____.
_{NOUN}

Later, he asked me for a/an _____
_{ADJECTIVE}

_____ to wrap around his neck and
_{NOUN}

_____ to warm his hands.
_{PLURAL NOUN}

The _____ sun was starting to make the
_{ADJECTIVE}

snowman feel a little sleepy. He said he needed to leave, but

promised to _____ again someday. I wiped
_{VERB}

a small _____ from the corner of my eye.
_{NOUN}

"_____!" I called to him as he shuffled away.
_{INTERJECTION}

That night, I opened our refrigerator for a/an

_____ glass of milk before bed, and there
_{ADJECTIVE}

was the snowman, sleeping comfortably next to the

_____!
_{PLURAL NOUN}

Knock! Knock!

Who's there?

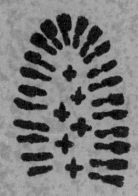

Phillip.

Phillip who?

Phillip your water bottle before a long hike.

Knock! Knock!

Who's there?

Gino.

Gino who?

Gino me after all this time, don't you?

Knock! Knock!

Who's there?

Ray.

Ray who?

Ray member my name, please!

Knock! Knock!
Who's there?
Zany.
Zany who?
Zany body home?

Ask a friend or family member for each of these words. Then use their words to fill in the silly story of Dr. Duh on the next page to create a Funny Fill-In to read aloud!

_____ NOUN	_____ ADJECTIVE
_____ NOUN	_____ ADJECTIVE
_____ NOUN	_____ ADJECTIVE
_____ NOUN	_____ VERB
_____ NOUN	_____ VERB
_____ PLURAL NOUN	_____ VERB
_____ PLURAL NOUN	

Dr. Duh

Dr. Duh was up to no good once again. He was building an

atomic _____, filled with
NOUN

_____. "With this invention," he cackled
PLURAL NOUN

fiendishly, "I shall take over the entire _____!"
NOUN

Using his supersonic listening abilities, Super Reader heard

Dr. Duh's _____ plan. Super Reader flew
ADJECTIVE

faster than a/an _____ _____ to
ADJECTIVE NOUN

Duh's lair.

"_____ at once, Duh!" cried Super Reader.
VERB

"Your _____ scheme has been thwarted!
ADJECTIVE

You're going to _____ in prison for a very
VERB

long time!"

"You'll never stop me!" cried Duh. And with that,

he began to _____ toward his
VERB

_____. Just when it seemed he would get
NOUN

away, Super Reader unplugged Duh's getaway

_____ and took Duh off to jail. Good
NOUN

_____ everywhere cheered!
PLURAL NOUN

What can you serve but never eat?

A tennis ball.

Why do ghosts make the best cheerleaders?

They've got spirit, yes they do!

What lights up the soccer stadium?

The match.

Why did Cinderella get kicked off the baseball team?

She kept running away from the ball!

What do baseball players use to bake a cake?

Batter, **bunt** pans, and oven **mitts.**

Ask a friend or family member for each of these words. Then use their words to fill in the silly story of Lake Monster on the next page to create a Funny Fill-In to read aloud!

_____ NOUN

_____ NOUN

_____ NOUN

_____ NOUN

_____ NOUN

_____ NOUN

_____ PLURAL NOUN

_____ ADJECTIVE

_____ ADJECTIVE

_____ ADJECTIVE

_____ ADJECTIVE

_____ VERB

_____ VERB

_____ VERB

Lake Monster

Last summer, we saw something very _____
ADJECTIVE
in the lake near our _____.
NOUN

We had taken out our _____ and were
NOUN
taking turns to _____ when Ryan
VERB
spotted something moving in the water.

We watched it for a long time. Sometimes it would

_____ the surface of the
VERB
_____ and then disappear completely.
NOUN

We had been fishing in the lake several times and had once

caught a/an _____
ADJECTIVE
_____ _____, but
ADJECTIVE   NOUN
this was much bigger.

Was it our very own Loch Ness monster? It seemed to

_____ closer towards us. We didn't
VERB
want to stick around to find out if it was a/an

_____.
NOUN

When we got back to our _____, we
NOUN
told our dad. "Oh yes," he said. "That old log has been

fooling people for many years now. It floats around looking

like _____ _____,
ADJECTIVE   PLURAL NOUN
and it fooled you, too!"

Knock! Knock!

Who's there?

Nana.

Nana who?

Nana your business!

Knock! Knock!

Who's there?

Turnip.

Turnip who?

Turnip your doorbell so you can hear it.

Knock! Knock!
Who's there?
Abby
Abby who?
Abby birthday to you!

Knock! Knock!
Who's there?
Eggs.
Eggs who?
Eggstremely surprised you don't know who it is!

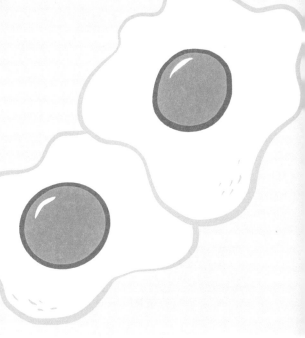

Knock! Knock!

Who's there?

Summer.

Summer who?

Summer here and summer there.

Knock! Knock!

Who's there?

Ben.

Ben who?

Ben knocking for quite a while!

Ask a friend or family member for each of these words. Then use their words to fill in the silly story of Crazy Cabin on the next page to create a Funny Fill-In to read aloud!

_____
NOUN

_____
NOUN

_____
NOUN

_____
NOUN

_____
NOUN

_____
NOUN

_____
NOUN

_____
PLURAL NOUN

_____
ADJECTIVE

_____
ADJECTIVE

_____
ADJECTIVE

_____
ADJECTIVE

_____
ADJECTIVE

_____
VERB

_____
PLURAL NOUN

Crazy Cabin

My Uncle Fred lives in a little _____ at the edge
NOUN
of a forest and a lake. It's no ordinary forest!

The last time I visited, instead of a dog, Uncle Fred had a pet
_____. It was well behaved, but it kept trying to
NOUN
_____ through the back door.
VERB

It began to rain one afternoon. Uncle Fred placed several
rusty buckets on the _____ and to my surprise,
NOUN
they were soon filled with _____
ADJECTIVE
_____.
PLURAL NOUN

I went for a ride in the _____ canoe one evening.
ADJECTIVE
I could hear the sound of _____ in the distance.
PLURAL NOUN
My _____ lantern didn't give off much
ADJECTIVE
_____.
NOUN
A large _____ swam under the canoe, bumping it
NOUN
and nearly tipping me into the _____
ADJECTIVE
_____. I saw a pair of glowing eyes moving
NOUN
towards me. But it turned out to be just a/an

_____ _____.
ADJECTIVE   NOUN

Why was the cheese in jail?

It had been up to no gouda.

Why was the grilled cheese sandwich crying?

It was having a total meltdown.

How do you get a mouse to smile for a photo?

Say cheese!

What is a basketball player's favorite kind of cheese?

Swish cheese!

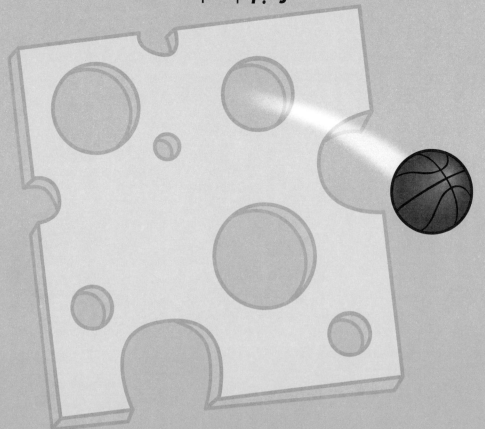

What kind of cheese surrounds a castle?

Moat-zarella.

Ask a friend or family member for each of these words. Then use their words to fill in the silly story of Summer in the Desert on the next page to create a Funny Fill-In to read aloud!

_____ NOUN	_____ ADJECTIVE
_____ NOUN	_____ ADJECTIVE
_____ NOUN	_____ VERB
_____ NOUN	_____ VERB
_____ PLURAL NOUN	_____ PLURAL NOUN
_____ PLURAL NOUN	_____ PLURAL NOUN

Summer in the Desert

Last summer, my family took a desert vacation. It was so

hot, _____ were melting and
<small>PLURAL NOUN</small>

small animals had to hide under _____
<small>PLURAL NOUN</small>

for shade.

The motel we stayed at wasn't the greatest. All the pool

water had evaporated, and it was filled with

_____. Instead of an air conditioner, each
<small>PLURAL NOUN</small>

room was cooled by _____ with fans.
<small>PLURAL NOUN</small>

That didn't help much.

We decided to sleep under the _____
<small>NOUN</small>

instead of in our stuffy motel room. We heard a coyote

_____ at the _____.
<small>VERB</small>   <small>NOUN</small>

The most amazing thing we saw was a talking

_____. It wore a/an
<small>NOUN</small>

_____ _____ and
<small>ADJECTIVE</small>   <small>NOUN</small>

spoke in a/an _____ voice, reminding us
<small>ADJECTIVE</small>

to drink lots of water.

When it began to _____ we all knew it
<small>VERB</small>

must be the heat playing tricks on us!

Knock! Knock!
Who's there?
Ants.
Ants who?
Knock! Knock!
Who's there?
Ants.
Ants who?
Knock! Knock!
Who's there?
Ants.
Ants who?
Knock! Knock!
Who's there?
Ants.
Ants who?
Knock! Knock!
Who's there?
Uncle.
Uncle who?
Uncle who is glad you got rid of all those ants!

Knock! Knock!
Who's there?
Sarah.
Sarah who?
Sarah phone I can use? My car's out of gas!

Knock! Knock!
Who's there?
Zaire.
Zaire who?
Zaire anyone home today?

Knock! Knock!
Who's there?
Watts.
Watts who?
Watts for dinner tonight?

Ask a friend or family member for each of these words. Then use their words to fill in the silly story of Split Pea Soup on the next page to create a Funny Fill-In to read aloud!

_____	_____
NOUN	ADJECTIVE
_____	_____
NOUN	ADJECTIVE
_____	_____
NOUN	VERB
_____	_____
NOUN	VERB
_____	_____
PLURAL NOUN	PLURAL NOUN
_____	_____
PLURAL NOUN	PLURAL NOUN

_____
PLURAL NOUN

Split Pea Soup

My grandma has a delicious recipe for split pea soup. Some

 people may not like it, but I sure do!

She starts with a cup of finely shredded _____

PLURAL NOUN

and a cup of _____ peas. She adds a pinch of

ADJECTIVE

_____ and a teaspoon of _____. The

NOUN — PLURAL NOUN

most surprising ingredient is a gallon of _____.

PLURAL NOUN

She stirs all the ingredients in a large _____ over

NOUN

medium heat. If they are in season, grandma adds some

fresh _____ and lets the soup simmer for a few

PLURAL NOUN

hours. This allows the _____ to blend nicely.

PLURAL NOUN

I told my grandma that she should sell the recipe to a big

_____ company or to a local restaurant. I am sure

NOUN

customers would _____ over it. People would

VERB

_____ from miles around to try this

VERB

_____ soup. But until that happens, I will fill a

ADJECTIVE

large _____ and enjoy it all by myself!

NOUN

Why was the math book so unhappy?

It had a lot of problems.

What do you call a kid with a dictionary in his or her pocket?

Smarty pants!

Why was the backpack always sleepy?

It was a napsack.

How many books can you put in an empty backpack?

Just one. After that, it's no longer empty!

Why did the kid throw out his alarm clock?

It kept going off each morning when he was sleeping!

Ask a friend or family member for each of these words. Then use their words to fill in the silly story of Lemonade Stand on the next page to create a Funny Fill-In to read aloud!

_____
NOUN

_____
NOUN

_____
NOUN

_____
PLURAL NOUN

_____
PLURAL NOUN

_____
PLURAL NOUN

_____
PLURAL NOUN

_____
PLURAL NOUN

_____
VERB

_____
VERB

_____
VERB

_____
ADJECTIVE

_____
ADJECTIVE

_____
ADJECTIVE

Lemonade Stand

One hot summer day, I decided to open a/an

_____ lemonade stand with the help of my
ADJECTIVE

younger brother, Liam. He was no help at all. Instead of

lemons, he put a/an _____ in the pitcher of
NOUN

water. And instead of writing LEMONADE FOR SALE on

the _____, he wrote
NOUN

_____ FOR SALE!
PLURAL NOUN

He spilled _____ all over the sidewalk and
PLURAL NOUN

tried to mop it up using a large _____.
NOUN

When I found _____ in the bag of lemons,
PLURAL NOUN

our day selling lemonade was done. It would take me

_____ to clean up the
PLURAL NOUN

_____ mess.
ADJECTIVE

I said, "You _____ right in the house and
VERB

stay there." I decided to go for a/an _____
VERB

to calm down.

Liam said he was sorry, so I smiled, and we decided to

_____ to the ice cream shop together. He said
VERB

he would pay for the ice cream _____, but I
PLURAL NOUN

paid instead. He's a pretty _____ little brother.
ADJECTIVE

Knock! Knock!

Who's there?

Althea.

Althea who?

Althea later. I gotta go now!

Knock! Knock!

Who's there?

Hans.

Hans who?

Hans off my candy bar!

Knock! Knock!

Who's there?

Butter

Butter who?

Butter open the door now if you want to find out!

Knock! Knock!
Who's there?
Banana.
Banana who?

Knock! Knock!
Who's there?
Banana.
Banana who?

Knock! Knock!
Who's there?
Banana.
Banana who?

Knock! Knock!
Who's there?
Banana.
Banana who?

Knock! Knock!
Who's there?
Lemon.
Lemon who?

Lemon know if you want another bunch of bananas!

Ask a friend or family member for each of these words. Then use their words to fill in the silly story of Dragon Day on the next page to create a Funny Fill-In to read aloud!

_____	_____
NOUN	PLURAL NOUN
_____	_____
NOUN	ADJECTIVE
_____	_____
NOUN	ADJECTIVE
_____	_____
NOUN	ADJECTIVE
_____	_____
NOUN	ADJECTIVE
_____	_____
NOUN	ADJECTIVE
_____	_____
PLURAL NOUN	VERB
_____	_____
PLURAL NOUN	FRIEND'S NAME
	_____
	FRIEND'S NAME

Dragon Day

King _____ declared that knights and dragons
fighting with each other had gone on for too long. He invited
all of his loyal _____ to the castle. He also invited
PLURAL NOUN
all the _____ dragons, too.
ADJECTIVE

"From this day forward, no _____ will ever harm
PLURAL NOUN
a/an _____ again," said the king. "Dragons will
NOUN
now _____ instead of breathing fire. And knights
VERB
will exchange their _____ swords for
ADJECTIVE
_____.
PLURAL NOUN

There was a/an _____ celebration in the kingdom.
ADJECTIVE
Knights and dragons feasted on _____
ADJECTIVE
_____ and sang _____ songs.
NOUN   ADJECTIVE

Princess _____ was very happy, as dragons had
FRIEND'S NAME
chased her to the _____ so many times.
NOUN

Unfortunately, the royal chef added too much pepper to the
_____. This caused the dragons to sneeze,
NOUN
blasting _____ and damaging the
NOUN
king's best _____.
NOUN

Why doesn't the sun go to college?

It already has millions of degrees!

What did one pig say to the other during the heat wave?

"I'm bacon!"

How can you keep lemons healthy in hot weather?

Give them lemon aid.

What holds the sun up in the sky?

Sunbeams.

What's black and white and red all over?

A panda with a sunburn.

Ask a friend or family member for each of these words. Then use their words to fill in the silly story of Science Fair Failures on the next page to create a Funny Fill-In to read aloud!

_____ NOUN

_____ NOUN

_____ NOUN

_____ NOUN

_____ PLURAL NOUN

_____ PLURAL NOUN

_____ ADJECTIVE

_____ ADJECTIVE

_____ ADJECTIVE

_____ ADJECTIVE

_____ ADJECTIVE

_____ ADJECTIVE

_____ ADJECTIVE

_____ ADJECTIVE

_____ VERB

_____ INTERJECTION

Science Fair Failures

About to walk home from _____ with his
                            NOUN
volcano, Jason saw Amy from his class putting her science fair

experiment in a/an _____
                        ADJECTIVE

_____.
       NOUN

"My science fair project was a flop," Amy said. "It was

supposed to be a/an _____ sunflower that
                         ADJECTIVE

turned _____. I placed it in a/an
              ADJECTIVE

_____ of water for seven whole days, but all
       NOUN

that happened was it got soggy!"

Jason shrugged and said, "My volcano didn't work, either. It's

so frustrating!" And Jason shook the _____
                                          ADJECTIVE

box angrily. Big mistake!

Inside the box was a jar containing _____
                                         ADJECTIVE

soap, red _____ _____,
                ADJECTIVE   PLURAL NOUN

vinegar, and baking soda. The ingredients spilled, mixed

together, and from the box spouted a/an

_____ _____ of foamy lava!
    ADJECTIVE   NOUN

" _____!" cried Jason, covered in
       INTERJECTION

_____ _____. "Just my
    ADJECTIVE   PLURAL NOUN

luck! NOW it works!" He and Amy laughed and began to

_____ home.
       VERB

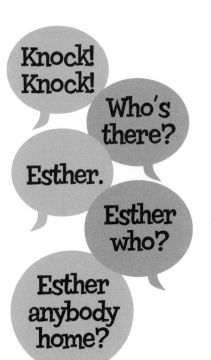

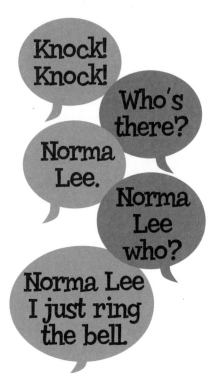

Knock! Knock!

Who's there?

Stopwatch.

Stopwatch who?

Stopwatch you're doing and open the door!

Ask a friend or family member for each of these words. Then use their words to fill in the silly story of The Strange Visitor on the next page to create a Funny Fill-In to read aloud!

_____
NOUN

_____
NOUN

_____
NOUN

_____
NOUN

_____
NOUN

_____
PLURAL NOUN

_____
PLURAL NOUN

_____
ADJECTIVE

_____
ADJECTIVE

_____
ADJECTIVE

_____
VERB

_____
VERB

_____
PLURAL NOUN

_____
PLURAL NOUN

The Strange Visitor

Boris had fallen asleep in his _____ reading one
NOUN

night. Around 2:00 a.m., a loud _____ startled
NOUN

him awake. The room was completely dark. "Who's there?"

cried Boris. A deep voice in the shadows replied, "It is I,

a _____ _____. And there is no
ADJECTIVE   NOUN

escaping my _____!"
PLURAL NOUN

Boris ran across the dark room and began to

_____ the stairs. But he felt a cold
VERB

_____ grip his ankle. He couldn't
NOUN

_____ at all!
VERB

"Wait!" shouted Boris. "If I give you my collection of

_____ _____, will you leave?"
ADJECTIVE   PLURAL NOUN

"You collect those, too?" said the voice. "That's amazing!

Do you also like to eat _____
ADJECTIVE

_____ on toast?"
PLURAL NOUN

"My favorite!" said Boris. He turned on the overhead

_____ and the two hairy monsters shook
NOUN

_____. "Nice to meet you! I'm Boris!"
PLURAL NOUN

What type of markets do dogs try to avoid?

What kind of kitten is very helpful in an emergency?

Why can't dogs watch movies at home?

Flea markets.

A first-aid kit.

They always hit the paws button.

How are dogs and cell phones the same?

They both have collar I.D.

REX

Who made this book?

Ultimate Super Silly Joke Book for Kids was made by the people who bring the weekly *Kid Scoop* page to hundreds of newspapers!

Kid Scoop believes learning is fun! Our educational activity pages teach and entertain. Teachers use the page in schools to promote standards-based learning. Parents use the *Kid Scoop* materials to foster academic success, a joy of learning, and family discussions. Our fun puzzles and activities draw children into the page. This stimulates a child's interest and they then read the text.

When Fox Chapel discovered *Kid Scoop*, they knew that there were lots of kids looking for books just like this one!

Vicki Whiting – Author

Vicki was a third-grade teacher for many years. Now she loves teaching kids through the weekly entertaining and educational *Kid Scoop* page. People often ask where she gets her ideas for each week's page. Vicki says, "I listen to the questions kids ask. We answer those questions with every *Kid Scoop* page!"

Jeff Schinkel – Illustrator

Jeff has loved to draw his whole life! As a kid, sometimes he was drawing when he should have been listening to the teacher in class. He earned a BFA in Illustration at the Academy of Art University in San Francisco, where drawing in class is highly encouraged. Jeff is now a member of the National Cartoonists Society.

Vivien Whittington – Operations Manager

Vivien is a voracious reader! She always wanted to work in publishing and after getting a degree in Fine Art, worked in publishing houses in London, England, starting as a researcher and leaving as a senior editor. Vivien coordinates the *Kid Scoop* team to complete around 50 different page deadlines a month—like an air traffic controller!

Eli Smith – Graphic Designer, Webmaster

Eli grew up in Cazadero, California, population 420, near the Russian River. He received a graphics degree from Santa Rosa Junior College and became interested in visual arts through his father, who is a painter. Eli is an accomplished photographer and spends weekends hiking and photographing the hills and beaches of Sonoma County.

Collect them all!

1

Super Silly Jokes for Kids
978-1-64124-067-3

2

Puzzling Pictures for Eagle-Eyed Kids
978-1-64124-066-6

3

Super Funny Knock Knock Jokes and
More for Kids - 978-1-64124-142-7

4

Super Fun Road Trip Activities for Kids
978-1-64124-240-0

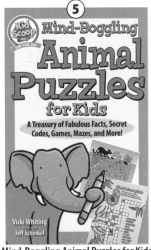

5

Mind-Boggling Animal Puzzles for Kids
978-1-64124-241-7

6

Awesome Funny Fill-Ins for Kids
978-1-64124-238-7

7

Brain-Bending Animal Puzzles for Kids
978-1-64124-242-4

8

Super Funny Fill-Ins for Kids
978-1-64124-239-4